Praying
Each Day
of the Year

Nicholas Hutchinson FSC

Matthew James Publishing Ltd

Also available:

1 898 366 30 6   Praying Each Day of the Year - volume 1: (January - April)

1 898 366 31 4   Praying Each Day of the Year - volume 2: (May - August)

First published 1998 by:

Matthew James Publishing Ltd,
19 Wellington Close, Chelmsford, Essex CM1 2EE

Reprinted 1999

ISBN: 1 898366 30 6

Cover design by Jez Coan
Printed by J W Arrowsmith Ltd., Bristol

Dedicated
to the memory of
Brother Damian Lundy, FSC
(1944-1996)
who shared the Good News with many
and bore sickness bravely.

Contents

Foreword

A warm welcome to those who have chosen to use this book! You are joining many others in different situations in schools, homes and parishes in reflecting and praying in a particular way each day of the year.

You are reading the first of three volumes that together offer for every day of the year a reflection and a prayer. The reflection is a "picture-story" - either a story itself or, more often, details of a specific event whose anniversary it is on that day. The accompanying prayer has been written around the theme. The book illustrates very practically how we can reflect on daily life and experiences and, living in God's Presence, can bring everything to him in prayer. It is hoped that the material may be of help in promoting a sense of reflection and prayerfulness that can pervade the day.

In 1997 a draft version of the book was used in different ways across the country in various schools, homes and parishes, but the book is written mainly for use by teachers in secondary schools. Teachers have "tried and tested" much of the material, and I have been very grateful for their comments and suggestions, as also those of various individuals who have used the draft version of the book for their personal reflection and prayer each day, especially several people who are seriously ill. Someone has remarked that "the reflective and prayerful approach of the book clearly proclaims that Jesus is the Way, the Truth and the Life".

Produced after much research, the book is offered primarily to busy Form Tutors who don't normally have much time or access to good resources to be producing more than a prayer as the *"daily act of collective worship"* for their own class at the start of each day. Teachers have commented already that this book offers ready-to-use quality material that helps to promote a sense of awareness, wonder and appreciation, that can contribute to the personal and spiritual development of individuals.

May all who use this book find help in reflecting and praying and walking in God's presence each day.

Introduction

The value of "picture-stories"

The most famous of all photographs of the Vietnam War was the horrific scene of several children suffering from the effects of napalm, pictured as they were running along a road, towards the camera. It is recognised that the photograph, taken in August 1972 and seen by millions throughout the world, was instrumental in bringing the war to an end. How powerful a picture can be! For hundreds of years, stained-glass windows presented picture-images mainly to those who could not read the Bible. Through her TV programmes and her books, Sister Wendy Becket has helped many people to *"really see"* and understand various meanings in paintings, illustrating the insight of D.H.Lawrence that *"the sense of wonder is the sixth sense, and it is the natural religious sense."* Saint Augustine has said that *"our whole business in this life is to restore to health the eye of the heart by which God may be seen"*, and we acknowledge that Christian education should promote in people *"a way of seeing"* (Evelyn Underhill), developing what William Blake calls *"the inward eye".*

Stories, too, can be "pictures" that convey a profound message, bringing it all alive. Aesop's fables have remained popular for 2,600 years. The Brothers Grimm recorded such stories as 'Little Red Riding Hood', teaching in a subtle way the need for personal safety. "Picture-stories" can also serve as "hooks" on which to "hang" what may be significant to an individual. Jesus told stories as a means of conveying the deep - yet simple - message of the Good News. That great story-writer, Charles Dickens, remarked that *"the Parable of the Prodigal Son is the best short story in the English language"* - not simply because of the poetry of the words, but because it is a timeless story that can reveal more each time it is heard. Some of Dickens' own stories portrayed a "hidden message" of the need for social change.

Some of the best stories are those that leave questions for the individual to ponder, and so can be more powerful in conveying a message than can an 'explanation' that attempts to summarise the message, just as adverts that leave something to the imagination are the most effective. It has been said that *"Jesus told stories and asked questions; we tend to moralise and give answers!"* It is hoped that each day's reflection and prayer will leave people with questions to ask of themselves in looking upon life critically and creatively, as well as leading them in ways of praying. The material in the book focuses on the specific rather than on what is general, and may encourage people to be reflective and prayerful based on the "here and now" of their daily lives. Some have commented that they have gained insights into how items from the news and newspapers can readily be turned to reflection and prayer.

Growing in awareness of the Presence of God

As the mind wanders during the day, it is likely that a recent "picture-story" is thought of again, encouraging the individual to reflect further. This thoughtfulness can, in turn, become part of a growing sense of being in the Presence of God. *"Prayer is about awakening to the Presence of God within us"* (Laurence Freeman), and *"the more we find Christ within, the more we become aware of Christ without"* (Bede Griffiths). As our young people are encouraged to acknowledge and recognise God's presence in themselves and in others, their lives and the lives of those around them will be enriched. It is true to say that the more we place ourselves in God's Presence, the more likely we are to have the same attitude and actions as Jesus: *"In his Presence we are bound to love"* (Evelyn Underhill).

The witness of reflection and prayer

Occasionally we experience or read about how an individual praying in great sincerity has a profound effect on others, and we can recall Pope Paul VI's memorable words:

People *"today listen more willingly to witnesses than to teachers, and if they do listen to teachers, it is because they are witnesses."*

(Evangelii Nuntiandi, 41)

Twice in his weekly articles in 'The Tablet', John Harriot reflected on Brother Alphonsus, a De La Salle Brother who had taught him. Harriot wrote of: *"the effect of seeing him pray and how he seemed to make God visible. Unobtrusively, unselfconsciously, the faith that inspired him was woven in and out of all we did. He was not given to pious exhortations. His pulpit was himself. Above all he was the kindest and gentlest of men."* ('The Tablet': 14/4/90). He went on to write about how Alphonsus was one of many who quietly and perseveringly lived his faith and made it real to all who came under his influence.

The crime-writer, Agatha Christie, wrote in her autobiography:

I can picture one teacher there - I can't recall her name.
She was short and spare, and I remember her eager jutting chin.
Quite unexpectedly one day
(in the middle, I think, of an arithmetic lesson)
she suddenly launched forth on a speech on life and religion.
"All of you," she said,
"every one of you, will pass through a time when you will face despair.

If you never face despair,
you will never have faced, or become, a Christian, or known a Christian life.
To be a Christian
you must face and accept the life that Christ faced and lived:
you must enjoy things as he enjoyed things,
be as happy as he was at the marriage at Cana,
know the peace and happiness that it means
to be in harmony with God and with God's will.
But you must also know, as he did,
what it means to be alone in the Garden of Gethsemane,
to feel that all your friends have forsaken you,
that those you love and trust have turned away from you,
and that God himself has forsaken you.
Hold on then to the belief that that is not the end.
If you love, you will suffer,
and if you do not love, you do not know the meaning of a Christian life."
She then returned to the problems of compound interest
with her usual vigour,
but it is odd that those few words,
more than any sermon I ever heard, remained with me
and, years later, they were to come back to me and give me hope
at a time when despair had me in its grip.
*She was a dynamic figure and also, I think, a **fine** teacher;*
I wish I could have been taught by her longer.

[Agatha Christie: 'An Autobiography'
(William Collins, 1977) page 150]

Both examples are of teachers who reflected on their personal experiences, and shared insights with the young people entrusted to their care - reflections that would bear fruit in years to come.

Good schools promote and cultivate goodness, and we are invited to fill our minds and share with others those things that are *"noble and good, praiseworthy and right, honourable and inspiring"* (Phil 4[4-9]). This book offers in a clear form many insights from our heritage that can be shared and passed on to others - insights that may be of lasting value to our students as they face the challenge to review their priorities. The reflections are presented in ways that attempt to engage interest and imagination during our *"daily act of collective worship"* in school (The Education Reform Act, 1988, s.6).

Some teachers will be of other than the Catholic faith, and some may choose to involve the students fully in the giving of the reflection and prayer. In time to come, the practice of reflecting and praying may develop in such a way that members of the school community from the youngest to the oldest may be able to share with others the fruits and insights of their own reflection and reading and life-experience and, in God's Presence, bring everything together in prayer. The following words of Pope Paul VI refer to people of all ages:

Above all, the Gospel must be proclaimed by witness.
Take a Christian, or a handful of Christians
who, in the midst of their own community,
show their capacity for understanding and acceptance,
their sharing of life and destiny with other people,
their solidarity with the efforts of all
for whatever is noble and good.
Let us suppose that, in addition,
they radiate in an altogether simple and unaffected way
their faith in values that go beyond current values,
and their hope in something that is not seen
and that one would not dare to imagine.
Through this wordless witness,
these Christians stir up irresistible questions
in the hearts of those who see how they live:
Why are they like this?
Why do they live in this way?
What or who is it that inspires them?
Why are they in our midst?
Such a witness is already
a silent proclamation of the Good News,
and a very powerful and effective one.

(Evangelii Nuntiandi, 21)

Young people need an experience of reflection and prayer.

In today's society with vast knowledge at our fingertips, we need to be careful to avoid "information overload". Peter Walker, a former Secretary of State for Wales, remarked that the hour he set aside every morning simply to reflect and "think his thoughts", with no distractions around him, enabled him to keep everything in perspective and be creative. That extraordinary man, Nelson Mandela, said: *"Although it was a tragedy to spend twenty-seven years in prison, one of the advantages was the ability to sit down and think. This is one of the things I miss most."*

The Book of Proverbs tells us that, *"Where there is no vision, the people perish"* (29[18]), reminding us of Plato's words that *"the unreflected life is not worth living."* Jesus *"offered reflections on every aspect of daily life",* Pope John Paul remarked during his visit to Scotland (1/6/82). The book illustrates how we can reflect on daily life. Reflections can then be brought together in prayer in the same way as the "collecting" of thoughts and intentions in the prayer that was once called the "Collect" in the Eucharist. The material in this book offers the all-important perspective of unity of life and human experience, seeking to integrate daily life rather than fragment and compartmentalise into "sacred" and "secular". Reflecting and praying may help to clarify our vision, review our priorities, and gain insights into how to learn from our experiences, as well as growing in Christ.

'Praying Each Day of the Year' may help in introducing some students to a spiritual life. Respecting the autonomy of each person, use of this book offers an experience of reflection and prayer in which some of the young people will participate fully. Some students may find it interesting or helpful to 'observe' people praying. Others may, in time, *"pray in their inner room"* (Mt 6^6) and *"seek first the kingdom of God"* (Mt 6^{33}). Some may take away "seeds" that may come to fruition only in the Lord's good time - not necessarily in ours!

The sharing of a reflection and prayer can be one of the means of Christian formation and a powerful means for people to grow. This particular sharing is an aspect of one of the key elements in pastoral care - wanting to *"be with"* the young people and hoping to *"touch (or win) their hearts",* offering an opportunity and an invitation to grow. The quality of a teacher's *"being with"* reflects the beliefs that the teacher has for the students, and has an impact on what the young people think of themselves. Indeed, one expression of *"invitational teaching"* is for the teacher to give his or her students *"a vision of their own greatness"* (Pullias).

"You send strange invitations, Sir," says Beauty in 'Beauty and the Beast'. Reflecting and praying with others can be a means of extending "invitations":

- invitations to grow in respect and appreciation of self and others;
- invitations to grow in responsibility, and serve those in need;
- invitations to grow in awareness and wonder, in understanding and wisdom (*"Wonder is the seed of knowledge"* remarked Francis Bacon);
- invitations to gain insights into what is of real value, and be life-affirming;
- invitations to discover *"the kingdom within",* seeking *"life in all its fullness"* as Jesus promised, becoming *"fully alive"* for the glory of God (cf. St Irenaeus).

Indeed, we read in *"The Common Good"* (of the Bishops' Conference of England and Wales, 1996 [37]) that

> *"it is the destiny and duty of each human being*
> *to become more fully human."*

Teaching itself is a way of *"being with"* people, and can include a mutual accompanying on the journey of growing in faith (cf. Emmaus: Lk 24[13-35]). Sometimes we have responded inadequately to young people's thirst for religious experience, yet *"it is necessary that the young know Christ who walks.... alongside each person as a friend"* (Pope John Paul II: 'Crossing the Threshold, p126). Use of this book offers an opportunity for people to walk in God's Presence.

Use in school

Many teachers will attest to the value of praying briefly **for** the students before praying **with** them - whether taking a moment to pray for them on the way to school or whilst walking to class, being conscious that *"if the Lord does not build the house, it is in vain that the builders labour."* (Ps 127[1]). We place our trust in the Lord to whom one of his friends said: *"Lord, teach us to pray"* (Lk 11[1]).

"The daily acts of collective worship" are part of the shared mission of the whole school community, whether they take place as class assemblies or larger group assemblies. As with various pastoral initiatives in secondary schools, if the sharing of a reflection and prayer is started as Year 7 arrive, they will assume it is the usual practice, and so will accept it as the norm for future years.

It is necessary to read through the material at least a day in advance. You may reflect on it personally yourself, and then have other ideas to contribute, so that it will become a personal reflection on your part. On days when it is decided to use the material in the format given, the numbering of each paragraph lends itself to the active participation of several people. If others are to be involved in the sharing of the reflection and prayer, you will want to encourage their preparation of the material in advance. Sometimes teachers take it for granted that readings will be presented clearly, with sufficient volume, and slowly enough! Do alert readers to any unusual words. The fact that students lead or present part of the reflection and prayer may also become one of the means for their growth in self-confidence and self-esteem.

If the prayer to be used is short, it is advisable for it to be written in advance on the board or for use with the overhead projector (prepared in either case before the students are in the room). A sense of involvement and participation and "ownership" is increased if everyone is invited to make such vocal prayer together, and we know that what is visual (in this case, the written word) is understood and retained much longer than what is simply heard. Such a visual stimulus encourages recall and further reflection later in the day.

Many of us have tended to limit ourselves to use only two or three 'formal' prayers as public prayer. Profound as those prayers are, the young people will not necessarily experience that prayer can be 'worded' in a way that is specific to situations in their daily lives. Prayer can be informal and familiar, and Carlo Carretto reminds us that *"prayer takes place in the heart, rather than in the head."* Deliberately the prayers here have not been written in formal or polished English, but generally in the style of spoken English. It is hoped that the style of the prayers will help promote the "speaking from the heart" that prayer is. Having read and used some of the prayers in this book, prayer-leaders may well feel encouraged to extemporise prayer in public, or write down words in advance that will be used as prayer.

On some days a quote or "punchline" may be repeated after the prayer - all the more effective if the prayer-leader avoids making an additional comment, thereby tending to elicit a personal response from some when recalled later in the day. To attempt to "preach" what kind of response there "should" be is likely to put people off and limit the action of the Holy Spirit!

Not all teachers fully appreciate that all the positive elements of a reflection and prayer can be negated by the attitude of one of the prayer-leaders or by the delivery or manner of delivery of comments or notices that might follow.

For those who wish (and have the time) to use the material more extensively (whether for a longer time in class, or for a year or school assembly), additional background information and some biblical references are included at the end of most days (📖). These details may help both teachers and students to introduce further ideas, and the cross-referring between some days may be of help. The additional background information is also there to help promote the thirst for knowledge, wisdom and understanding in the young people who themselves read the material, possibly following up by using CD-ROM encyclopedias, etc.

Teachers will find that materials set out for weekends and for holiday times - particularly the month of August - will provide further resource material for use on school days!

For year or school assemblies, some hymns are listed to offer a ready choice, suitable to the theme of the day (🎼). Occasionally reference is made to a poem. Such poems are the more commonly known and, for convenience, all are to be found in *"The Nation's Favourite Poems"* (BBC Books 0-563-38782-3), being a compilation of the nation's top 100 favourite poems, according to a Radio 4 nationwide poll in 1995.

'Praying Each Day of the Year' is printed in three conveniently-sized volumes. At the back of the appropriate volume appear materials for such "movable feasts" as Ash Wednesday, the days of Holy Week, Pentecost, and Family Fast Days. The book's comprehensive index should help to locate themes, people, and particular passages, especially if you recall only a few key words of a familiar passage.

Many will find very useful a resource that is printed at the back of Volume 1 - *"Locating passages in the Bible".* Here are references to some 600 key events and writings from both the Old and the New Testaments, listed in a very clear and user-friendly way. Too often we have thought of a passage but have been unable to locate it! Many of the prayers in the book have drawn their inspiration from scripture.

At the back of Volume 2 is a collection of prayers for use by teachers for colleagues and students. These have been "tried and tested" by several schools which now choose one of these (or other) prayers for staff briefings and meetings, for the daily or weekly staff briefing sheet, for the monthly newsletter to parents, or for such occasions as the annual parent-governor meeting. Individual teachers have used the collection as a means of praying for colleagues and for particular students.

Volume 3 concludes with a selection of further ideas for helping to lead the young people in reflection and prayer, as well as various means for helping in class to recall that we are in the Presence of God.

As you take up this book each day, it will be in the spirit of all that is presented here if, briefly, you think and pray for all others in different schools and situations who will be using the same material as you. Do pray that we may all become more reflective and prayerful and *"fully alive"* because we have shared an experience of something of God's love. And so may all of us who use this book - fellow pilgrims on the road to Emmaus - each be able to share our own story of what happens to us on our journey through life, and how we recognise Jesus in our midst.

Brother Nicholas Hutchinson, FSC
De La Salle House,
83 Carr Lane East,
Liverpool L11 4SF

Praying
Each Day
of the Year

(See also 16 January)

1 The people of Ancient Rome thought there were many gods, and the month of January is named after 'Janus', their god of doors and gateways, of beginnings and endings. In Rome, the temple of Janus had doors facing east and west for the rising and setting of the sun, the beginning and end of each day. Between those doors stood the statue of Janus with two faces, looking in opposite directions.

2 As we start the New Year, looking both backwards and forwards, we can think of the new year as a gate - an opening - to what we choose to do in the future. The darkness of winter and of past mistakes will give way to the light of spring and of new opportunities.

3 In the dark days of World War II, with the whole country "blacked out" at night to deter enemy bombing, King George VI *(the sixth)* gave a glimmer of hope to people as he spoke these words:

4 *'I said to the man*
who stood at the gate of the Year:
"Give me a light
that I may tread safely into the unknown."
And he replied:
"Go out into the darkness
and put your hand into the hand of God.
That shall be to you
better than light,
and safer than a known way.
May that almighty hand
guide and uphold us all." '

5 *Let us pray:*

Lord Jesus,
at this time
we can look back to the old year,
and forward to the new.

We give thanks
for the blessings of the past year,
and we place into your hands
the mistakes we have made.
As you are "the Light of the world",
take away the darkness in our lives.
As you are "the Way",
lead us in the year ahead.
As you are "the gate of the sheepfold",
protect us from danger.
We entrust the past to your mercy, Lord,
the present to your love,
and the future to your providence.
Amen.

📖 *"light of the world" - Jn 8^{12};*
"Way, Truth and Life" - Jn 14^6;
"gate" - Jn 10^9;
"past, present, future" - St Augustine.

📖 *For an alternative prayer see 4 March*

📖 *'Janus', the god of beginnings and endings, would be addressed in prayer by families at the start of each day. He was also invoked at the start of wars, throughout which his temple doors would be kept open in Rome. Coming from the word "Janus" we have "janitor", being a doorkeeper, a porter.*

📖 *The quote of King George VI [the father of Queen Elizabeth II] is from the writings of Minnie Haskins, and was broadcast by the King on Christmas Day, 1939. The last two lines printed here were not broadcast but, for completion's sake, are included as they are the full words of the author.*

🎵 Christ be beside me; Father I place into your hands; I heard the Lord call my name; Oh the love of my Lord; This day God gives me.

1 On 4th January 1809, Louis Braille was born in Paris. His father used leather to make harnesses for horses. When Louis was very young, he was playing in his father's workshop, and he pressed an awl against some leather to try to make a hole. The awl slipped and struck his eye. Before long, his other eye became infected and he became totally blind.

2 He attended a school for the blind in Paris. Large letters were raised on each page so that the person could recognise words by moving a finger over the large letters. Louis thought back to how his father worked, remembering that the awl would make a small lump on the other side of the leather before making a hole. He realised that he could press on one side of a sheet of paper to make raised dots on the other side. Aged 15, he set about devising a code of letters that we now know as the Braille system of printing and writing for the blind.

3 Each letter is represented by a combination of raised dots - up to a maximum of six, laid out two across and three down.

4 *Let us pray:*

Lord Jesus, light of the world,
 open our eyes
 to notice the magnificence
 of creation.
Open our eyes
 that we may always
 value and appreciate
 all who are part of our lives.
Open our eyes
 that we may be quick to notice
 when people are going through
 difficulties.
Open our eyes
 so that we may share your vision
 and "really see". Amen.

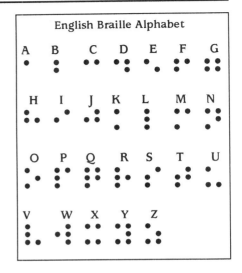

English Braille Alphabet

📖 *Louis Braille: 4/1/1809 - 6/1/1852*

📖 *Some restaurants [e.g. Henry's Table] have a braille menu on request.*

📖 *After the 1997 General Election, David Blunkett, who is blind, was appointed Secretary of State for Education and Employment. All of his papers needed to be prepared in Braille. The red boxes/cases in which ministers receive their papers were too small for David Blunkett's Braille papers, and so slightly larger ministerial red boxes were made for him.*

📖 *See also 'Helen Keller': 1/3 June*

📖 *John 9 - Jesus' cure of the man born blind. St John links this miracle with the Jewish leaders who were "blind" as to who Jesus was.*

🎼 Amazing grace; Christ is our king, let the whole rejoice; I saw the grass; Walk with me, oh my Lord.

1 On this day in 1944 occurred one of the worst-ever train disasters - over 500 people were killed. It wasn't a crash, and the train wasn't even moving when the people died.

2 The passenger train had many carriages and a steam engine at each end in case one broke down, but there was no communication system between the two engines.

3 The train had entered the El Toro Tunnel in Leon, in northern Spain, when the front engine stopped and the train came to a halt. The engine at the back had just entered the tunnel. Presuming that the front engine was no longer able to pull the train, the engine at the other end started up, ready to back out of the near end of the tunnel.

4 At the very same time, the front engine managed to start up again. Each engine was then trying to pull the train in opposite directions within the tunnel, neither realising that the other engine had started up. Both drivers simply thought that more power was needed to pull the lengthy train, and so put more and more coal into the furnace of each of the steam engines. Gases from burning the coal, of course, left the funnel of each of the engines. The gases - particularly carbon monoxide - built up in the tunnel as the two engines opposed each other. The gases soon poisoned and killed over five hundred passengers.

5 In our prayer we can bring to mind people who experience stress and tension in their daily lives, feeling pulled in different directions:

- families that are torn apart;
- countries where there is civil war, and neighbours who fight each other;
- those who have to consider different viewpoints and then make decisions that will affect many people;
- those people whom disaster, trauma and difficulties have torn apart.

6 *Let us pray:*

If the word "compassion", Lord, means "to suffer with", lead us to be ready to stand beside those who suffer. Amen.

✍ *Alternative prayer: as for 11 January re 'Journey'.*

✍ *Matthew 6²⁴: No-one can be the slave of two masters (being "pulled" in different directions; we can't have it both ways.)*

✍ *2 Cor 1³⁻⁷ - from our suffering we can comfort others.*

🎵 Father, I place into your hands; There is a world

4 JANUARY

(See 2 January for Louis Braille)

(See also 20 March for Isaac Newton)

1 Isaac Newton was born on January 4th 1643. What is Newton remembered for?

2 He developed Calculus, a branch of mathematics.

3 In studies of light, he showed via a prism that sunlight is made of a spectrum of colours - red, orange, yellow, green, blue, indigo, violet.

4 Newton formulated Three Laws of Motion, which led to his theory of Universal Gravitation (often remembered in the incident of the falling apple).

5 Newton's work was a turning point in science, but he acknowledged that his progress and success were built on the hard work and achievements of people before him:

"If I have seen further, it is by standing on the shoulders of giants."

6 *Let us pray:*

Lord,
  there is so much that I don't know,
  and I ask you to inspire me
  with a thirst for knowledge.
I pray, too,
  for wisdom and understanding
  that I may use my knowledge well.
I give thanks
  for many people I have never met
  whose knowledge
  and understanding
  have been passed on to me.
I ask that I may benefit
  from their work and experience
  and may contribute, in turn,
  to the well-being of others. Amen.

📖 *The quote, "Standing on the shoulders of giants", is from a letter that Newton wrote to fellow-scientist, Robert Hooke, 5/12/1676.*

📖 *Newton also said:*
"I do not know what I may appear to the world, but to myself I seem to have been only a boy playing on the seashore, and diverting myself in now and then finding a smoother pebble or a prettier shell than ordinary, whilst the great ocean of truth lay all undiscovered before me."

📖 *Reference books in countries other than Britain give Newton's date of birth as 4/1/1643, which is according to the Gregorian Calendar by which we now live. It was the Julian Calendar that was being followed in Newton's time in Protestant England, whilst the Catholic mainland of Europe had adopted the Gregorian Calendar when proposed by Pope Gregory XIII (13th) in 1582. According to the Julian Calendar (as in England) Newton's date of birth would have been 25/12/1642.*

📖 *Newton developed Calculus at the same time as Gottfried Leibniz developed it independently in Germany.*

📖 *1 Kings 3$^{5-14}$ - King Solomon asks for wisdom.*

🎼 Oh the love of my Lord is the essence.

(See also 6/7 January and 25 July)

1   Two thousand years ago, a visit to a Greek town by government representatives was known as an "epiphany". It is a Greek word that describes an appearance, manifestation, or revelation of someone important arriving amongst the people.

2   The word "Epiphany" has been used for the last two thousand years to describe God coming closer to the people, revealing himself in his Son, Jesus. The Feast of the Epiphany (on the 6th January) celebrates the Wise Men from the East recognising Jesus for who he is, and giving him their gifts of gold, frankincense, and myrrh.

3   In the final verse of the hymn, "In the bleak mid-winter", we hear the words:
"What can I give him, poor as I am?
If I were a shepherd I would bring a lamb;
if I were a wise man I would do my part,
yet what I can I give him - give my heart."

4. We can focus today on the gift of **GOLD**, knowing that it represents what is special. Special jewellery is made from gold. *"Hearts of Gold"* has been a popular TV programme, celebrating how people with *"hearts of gold"* have helped others.

5. I can think of special people and things in my life that are **GOLD** for me. I can stand with the wise men and offer what I think is "gold" in my life:
    - my talents;
    - happy memories;
    - times when everything has gone well;
    - what I enjoy;
    - my friends;
    - times when someone has encouraged me;
    - what I look forward to.

6   *Let us pray:*

Lord, I give thanks
for the "gold" in my life:
for the people who are precious to me,
for the happy memories I treasure,
and for all that has been good
over the years.
May all that has been "gold" for me,
remind me always to appreciate
all who are part of my life.
Inspire me, Lord,
to live in such a way
that I help to bring out the best
in others.
Amen.

You could have before you something that is made of gold or is gold-plated.

We can read about the visit of the Wise Men in St Matthew's gospel, Mt 2^{1-12}. "Gentiles" is a word meaning "all who are not Jews". The Wise Men, as Gentiles, symbolise that Jesus, the Son of God, has come for all people and not just for the Jewish people. N.B. they are not called "Three Kings" in the Gospel; that thought comes from our carols and from imagery in Psalm 71/72.

"Epiphany" means "revelation" or "manifestation". A "manifest" is a list that reveals the details of the cargo on a ship or aeroplane.

 In the bleak midwinter

6 JANUARY

(See also 5/7 January, and 25 July)

1 If people with toothache cannot see the dentist quickly, they can take various things to help kill the pain - such as a paracetamol tablet, or a liquid dabbed on to the tooth called "oil of cloves". Some chemist shops sell "tincture of myrrh", which is a liquid with myrrh dissolved in it. Dabbed on to a tooth, myrrh can ease the pain of toothache.

2 In Saint John's Gospel we read that, after the death of Jesus, his body was washed and anointed with sweet-smelling spices and herbs, including myrrh. (Jn 19^{39})

3 We can think of myrrh, then, as representing pain and sorrow and death. I can think of what might be the **MYRRH** in my own life - the sorrows and pain and difficulties I have experienced:
- not-so-good things;
- being ill;
- feeling under pressure or stress;
- having made mistakes and having failed;
- when things haven't gone well;
- falling out with others;
- feeling down or rejected;
- sad and difficult times.

4. *Let us pray:*

Lord Jesus,
   you call me to live
   every aspect of my life
   in your presence,
   and so I come before you as I am.
With the myrrh
   that the wise men carried
   I bring, too,
   the pain and sorrow and suffering
   that I have experienced.
I lay them before you
   because they are all part of who I am.

I ask that good may come
   from whatever negative things
   happen to me,
   knowing that nothing
   can ever separate me from your love.
Amen.

📖 *The four gospels vary about the details of Jesus being offered something to drink before or during his crucifixion. Mark's gospel [15^{23}] records that Jesus, just before being crucified, turned down the offer of wine mixed with myrrh. As the myrrh would have helped to deaden some of the pain, perhaps this was a sign of Jesus wanting to identify fully with so many people who find that suffering is part of their lives.*

📖 *Myrrh comes from the sap which oozes out of a bush. It solidifies into an oily yellow gum with a sweet smell. Because of its sweet smell, myrrh has been used in perfumes and cosmetics.*

📖 *Gold, frankincense and myrrh are often thought of as the gifts to Jesus as King, Priest and Prophet, respectively.*

📖 *Epiphany is sometimes known as "Twelfth Night", as it starts on the 12th night after Christmas. It is the title of one of Shakespeare's plays, in which we read: "Be not afraid of greatness: some men are born great, some achieve greatness, and some have greatness thrust upon them." - Act II, Scene V, line 158.*

🎵 All that I am; Come and join the celebration; In the bleak mid-winter; Sing a simple song; The first Nowell

JANUARY 7

(See also 5/6 January, and 25 July)

1 The Wise Men came from the lands that are to the East of Palestine. One of the main routes was called "the Incense Road" because merchants travelled along it with expensive incense and myrrh, sometimes exchanging them for gold.

2 **FRANKINCENSE** (often simply called "incense") is a gum that comes from a tree. When added to a flame or very hot charcoal, sweet-smelling smoke comes off and rises in the air. One of the psalms in the Bible talks of *"my prayer rising before you, Lord, like incense."* Sometimes in church, incense is burned as a sign of prayer and offering. Incense is often used at funerals , reminding us in prayer that the ordinary person is also very special.

3 If **GOLD** stands for the special things in life, and **MYRRH** represents the sorrow and difficulties, then **INCENSE** can stand for something in-between. The *ordinary* things of life can become *special* (depending on my attitude and how I go about them) - such ordinary things as:

- getting up;
- cooking, eating, and clearing up after meals;
- housework;
- going to school or work;
- helping somebody who doesn't seem grateful.

4 All these "ordinary" things of life I can transform by a positive attitude.

5 *Let us pray:*

Lord, as I offer you
  all that is ordinary
  and everyday in my life,
  I ask you
  to give me the power of your Spirit
that I may transform each day
by living with a positive attitude,
looking for the best
in people and situations.
Inspire me to live in your presence
every day
so that I may share your outlook
and do the ordinary things of life
in an extraordinary way.
May this, Lord, my prayer today,
rise before you
like the burning of incense.
Amen.

6 There is a saying:

*"Wise men followed Jesus.
People who are wise still do."*

📖 *"Let my prayer rise before you like incense"* - Psalm 141 [140].

📖 *"Make your lives extraordinary"* - a phrase used by the teacher, Mr Keating [Robin Williams], in the film, *"The Dead Poets' Society"*.

📖 Poem: *"A cold coming we had of it"* - T S Eliot.

🎵 All that I am; Come and join the celebration; In the bleak midwinter; Sing a simple song; The first Nowell.

8 JANUARY

1   In 1989 a spacecraft called 'Galileo' was launched on a journey to the planet Jupiter. The craft was named after the astronomer, Galileo, who died on this day in 1642.

2   Using a telescope, Galileo (the astronomer) discovered four moons orbiting the planet Jupiter. We now know that Jupiter has at least 16 moons. The largest moon, Callisto, is larger than the planet Mercury.

3   Jupiter itself is 1400 times the volume of our own planet Earth. Whilst the Earth is 150 million km (93 million miles) from the Sun, Jupiter's orbit is five times that distance from the Sun.

4   *Let us pray:*

Lord God,
   may all of your creation
   - from the vastness
      of mighty planets and stars
   to the lowliness
      of the smallest living creature
      I can see
   - remind me
   to live in wonder and appreciation
   of all that is around me. Amen.

Galileo Galilei: 15/2/1564 - 8/1/1642. It was on 7/1/1610 that he discovered the 4 moons. He named them Io, Europa, Ganymede, and Callisto. Collectively these four are now known as "the Galilean Moons".

Jupiter radiates twice as much energy as it receives from the Sun. Using mathematical equations, scientists can calculate the mass of Jupiter. Knowing its volume and mass, its density can then be worked out - being a quarter that of Earth. Accordingly Jupiter can't be made of the rocks and metals that Earth is, but must be made of gases.

N.A.S.A.'s Voyager 1 and Voyager 2 spacecraft passed Jupiter in 1979, providing much information about the planet. In July 1994, fragments of the Shoemaker-Levy 9 Comet crashed into the planet.

Ps 104 [103], Psalm 8 [see 12 April].

Oh Lord my God, the Father of creation; O Lord my God, when I in awesome wonder; Yahweh I know you are near.

(See 12 January for the rescue of the sailor, Tony Bullimore.)

(See also 11 March re Dr Alexander Fleming.)

1   In his laboratory in St Mary's Hospital, London, Doctor Alexander Fleming was breeding some germs for his research. In a small round dish he was growing some staphylococcus bacteria - the cause of a number of diseases from boils to pneumonia.

2   When Fleming returned from holiday on this day in 1928 he saw that the lid of one of his bacteria cultures had fallen off. What looked like a bit of fluff had landed on the plate - it was some fungus that had blown in through the open window. Around that fungus all the bacteria had stopped growing or had been killed. The green fungus looked like mould on stale food, and Fleming set out to grow it by feeding it on more of the bacteria. He identified the fungus as a mould called 'penicillium notatum'.

3   Fleming's laboratory assistant had a sinus infection. Knowing that this mould had killed off the bacteria that caused various illnesses, the lab assistant volunteered to take some of the mould. His health improved.

4   In 1940, just after the start of the Second World War, two scientists working in Oxford isolated the active ingredient in that fungus, and called the medicine "penicillin", after the name of the mould. Penicillin was not harmful to humans, and it saved the lives of many soldiers during the Second World War. Powdered penicillin was sprinkled into the open wounds of soldiers who would otherwise have died. Penicillin can also be given in tablet form, or can be injected. It became known as "the miracle drug" and it has saved the lives and suffering of many people since then.

5   Sir Alexander Fleming and the two other scientists were awarded a Nobel Prize in 1945. Fleming remembered how the fungus had blown in through his open window onto a plate whose top had fallen off. He acknowledged that chance and co-incidence had played a great part in this great discovery. He said: *"There are thousands of different moulds, and there are thousands of different bacteria. It was chance that that mould was in the right place at the right time."*

6   *Let us pray:*

Lord, give us each day
   the wisdom to recognise
   which things are important,
   and which things are not.
Show us how best
   to use the time and talents
   you have given us.
Help us to use all opportunities wisely
   that we may give in service to others
   the good gifts we have received
   from you. Amen.

📖 *Alexander Fleming: 6/8/1881 - 11/3/1955*

📖 *The two scientists who contributed to the development of penicillin were Howard Florey and Ernst Chain. The three together received the Nobel Prize in 1945.*

📖 *On 11/7/97 a sample of the mould from which Sir Alexander Fleming had discovered penicillin was auctioned at Christie's in London, fetching £14,950. The mould, stored in a wooden box with an inscribed brass plate, was bought for the Science Museum in London.*

1 All British stamps bear the head of the Queen or King reigning at the time. Other than that, what is unique about British stamps compared with those of all other countries?

2 Stamps of every country - except Britain - bear the name of the country. When stamps first appeared, there was no need to include the country's name to distinguish them from stamps of other countries, since only Britain was then producing stamps.

3 On this day in 1840, Rowland Hill introduced a system of paying to the Post Office a penny for a stamp which would be stuck on the envelope. The penny stamp would cover costs of delivery of letters throughout the United Kingdom. Before that time it would be the person receiving a letter who had to pay.

4 When letters were delivered, time was being wasted in waiting for people to answer the door. Another invention of Rowland Hill then, was to have a slit in doors through which letters could be put - hence our letter boxes in doors.

5 *Let us pray:*

**Commemorative stamps, Lord,
call to mind famous people,
sport and inventions,
and nature, art and history.
As I value what these images represent,
lead me particularly, Lord,
to value every individual person
- made as we all are
in your image and likeness.
Inspire me to show appreciation
to all who are a part of my life.
May I use well
all the opportunities that come my way
to make my part of the world
a better place. Amen.**

📟 *Our modern decimal currency is of 100 pennies to the pound. Until 15/2/1971 there were 12 pennies in a shilling [our 5p] and 20 shillings in a pound - 240 pennies making a pound. In 1995 a stamp commemorating Rowland Hill and the one penny postage cost 25 pence - the equivalent of 60 pennies of the currency of Hill's time.*

📟 *Sir Rowland Hill, 1795-1879, was a teacher and a civil servant. He is buried in Westminster Abbey.*

📟 *Portraits of living people are forbidden on U.S. stamps.*

 I will never forget you.

1 Whilst London's rapid transport system is called "the Underground" or "the Tube", the system in Paris is known as "the Metro".

2 Yesterday is the anniversary, in the year 1863, of the opening in London of the world's first underground railway system. London Underground is the world's longest - over 250 miles (400 kms) in length.

3 *Let us pray*
for all who will be making journeys today:

We pray, Lord,

- for those who are going to a new job and for those who are going to work for the last time today;
- for the emergency services who will travel at high speed on land, water or in the air, to bring help to others;
- for those starting a new life as they move house;
- for those travelling to or from prison;
- for people who will go into hospital today;
- for young people on their way to school, college and university;
- for those who are lost on the journey of life;
- for those who will die today and make their final journey.

On all these people we ask your blessing, Lord. Amen.

📖 *The first part of the Underground opened was a section of what is now called the Metropolitan Line, between Paddington and Farringdon Street.*

📖 *Paris' metro is half the length of the London Underground, but carries more passengers. San Francisco's rapid transport system is called "BART" - "The Bay Area Rapid Transport".*

🎵 Father, in my life I see; I am the way;
Moses I know you're the man;
Walk with me.

1 The British yachtsman, Tony Bullimore, sailed in the Whitbread round-the-world yacht race in his boat, 'Exide Challenger'. Horrendous sea conditions between Australia and the Antarctic caused his boat to capsize, to overturn. An automatic satellite distress signal was picked up from the upturned boat, but he was nearly 1500 miles from the nearest land, Australia. Satellite technology enabled the Australians to locate the boat, and they sent spotter planes to keep it in sight. No-one knew, though, if Tony Bullimore was still alive.

2 Because of the huge distances involved, it took three days for the Australian Navy in their ship, the 'Adelaide', to reach the stricken yacht. On the 9th January 1997, a dinghy from the 'Adelaide' took a few men across to Bullimore's boat. There they hammered on the upturned yacht. A few seconds later, Tony Bullimore emerged from the water to cheers from the navy.

3 He had survived by crouching on a shelf, with nets stretched across to stop himself falling into the ice-cold water inside the upside-down boat. He was in total darkness for those three days, with his boat still being buffeted by 60 foot waves. Not being able to see outside, he suffered from motion sickness and, hearing creaking of the hull, he was never sure if the boat would break up.

4 Parts of some of his fingers were later amputated because of the damage from the severe cold. Tony Bullimore would not have survived without his protective survival clothes, and he had a little chocolate to eat and fresh water to drink. *"It was a miracle"*, he said, *"an absolute miracle. I got to the point where I was thinking in hours. I feel that I've been born again."*

5 Across the world, the Australian Navy and Air Force were praised for their skills and courage and determination in the rescue.

6 *Let us pray:*

**We pray, Lord, for all
who will need strength and courage
in the day ahead:**
- **for those who face danger;**
- **for those who risk themselves
for others;**
- **for those who must make
an important decision today;**
- **for people who are seriously ill;**
- **for those facing persecution
or torture.**
**We ask you, Lord,
to give them
the power of your Spirit.
Amen.**

📖 *We can reflect individually as to how fragile we are. The following prayer is that of a fisherman from Brittany in France, and a copy of the prayer was kept on the desk of U.S. President Jimmy Carter (1977–1981), and is used by some teachers with newcomers to the school:*
> *"Lord, the sea is so big
> and my boat is so small.
> Be with me."*

📖 *Psalm 106/107$^{23-32}$*
  - Some sailed to the sea in ships

📖 *Poem: "Sea-fever" by John Masefield.*

📖 *Song: "I'm born again" by Boney M*

♩ Amazing grace; Be not afraid; Do not be afraid; Eternal Father, strong to save (for those in peril on the sea); I am with you for ever; I will be with you; The light of Christ; Yahweh I know you are near.

1. The greatest goal difference between two teams in an FA Cup Final was 6-0 for Bury against Derby County in 1903.

2. Which is the only English town whose team is in the Scottish Football League?

3. The answer is Berwick-upon-Tweed. It is a town on the North Sea coast on the English/Scottish border. It changed hands 13 times between England and Scotland, until finally resting with England in 1482.

4. Someone has compared LIFE with a football game, and has written these words about the way we live:

5. *"For when the One Great Scorer comes*
To write against your name,
He marks - not that you won or lost,
But how you played the game."

6. *Let us pray:*

Lord our God,
may the playing
and the watching of sport
remind me
of the qualities I need for living:
  developing skills and talents,
  appreciating the different skills
    that others have,
  learning to co-operate with others,
  being positive,
  having respect for others,
  being determined and committed,
  having a clear goal at which to aim.
Inspire me to work hard
  at developing these qualities
  in daily life
  so that each of us - working together -
  may help to build up your Kingdom.
Amen.

In 1147 it was decided that the River Tweed would be the English/Scottish border.

The "One Great Scorer" quote is by Grantland Rice, 1880-1954

Father, in my life I see; Father I place into your hands; I give my hands; Take my hands.

14 JANUARY

(See also 4 September)

1 Albert Schweitzer was born on this day in 1865. He became a world-famous organist and author, and sacrificed a comfortable life in France and Germany to be a missionary doctor. In Africa he set up a hospital and leper-colony for the very poor.

2 He encouraged others to share his *"reverence for life"*, growing in compassion for life in all its forms. He wrote:

"By having reverence for life, we enter into a spiritual relationship with the world."

He helped lead others to see that, with love and compassion and respect for all life, people would find a greater meaning in their lives. In 1952 Doctor Albert Schweitzer was awarded the Nobel Peace Prize.

3 We can use a short prayer of his today - a prayer of offering. It's the kind of prayer some people memorise and use from time to time:

4 **"Here, Lord, is my life.
I place it on the altar today.
Use my life as you will."**

📖 *After many setbacks, Albert Schweitzer built up a hospital and leper-colony in Lambaréné in French Equatorial Africa [now in the country of Gabon on the west coast of Africa].*

📖 *Albert Schweitzer was born on 14/1/1875 in Alsace, formerly French territory which had become part of Germany. In the last years of the First World War he was interned in France because he was German-born. He died on 4/9/1965.*

📖 *See 28 April for an alternative prayer.*

🎵 All that I am; Do not worry; Father I place into your hands; Follow me; Here I am, Lord; If I am lacking love; I give my hands; Take my hands.

(See also 4/5 April)

1 Martin Luther King, the American Civil Rights leader, was born on this day in 1929 in Atlanta, Georgia, in the southern United States.

2 In the United States in 1955, people were still kept apart because of the colour of their skin. Only whites could sit at the front of buses, for example, and if all the places for white people were occupied, it was the law that black people would have to stand and give up their seat for the whites. On 1st December 1955 a black lady, Mrs Rosa Parks, refused to give up her place, and she was arrested.

3 Martin Luther King was one of the Christian leaders who opposed the laws and the attitude of discrimination, and he would eventually pay for it with his life, even though he was fully committed himself to non-violence. He said: *"Love is the only force capable of transforming an enemy into a friend."*

In 1963 in Birmingham, Alabama, people promised non-violence by signing a pledge which made 10 points:

4 *"I hereby pledge myself to the non-violent movement. Therefore I will keep the following ten commandments:*

  1 *MEDITATE daily on the teachings and life of Jesus.*

  2 *REMEMBER always that the non-violent movement seeks justice and reconciliation - not victory.*

  3 *WALK and TALK in the manner of love, for God is love.*

  4 *PRAY daily to be used by God in order that all people might be free.*

  5 *SACRIFICE personal wishes in order that all people might be free.*

  6 *OBSERVE with both friend and foe the ordinary rules of courtesy.*

  7 *SEEK to perform regular service for others and for the world.*

  8 *REFRAIN from the violence of fist, tongue or heart.*

  9 *STRIVE to be in good spiritual and bodily health.*

  10 *FOLLOW the directions of the movement and of the steward on a demonstration.*

I sign this pledge, having seriously considered what I do, and with the determination and will to persevere."

5 *Let us pray:*

Father, may our human family
   not become separated from you
   by building barriers of race or colour,
   of religion or class.
Inspire us to recognise
   that we are all made
   in your image and likeness,
   so that we may grow in appreciation
   of all people,
   and encourage each other
   to grow in pride in who we are
   and who we are called to be.
May we recognise your Son in our midst,
   and live truly as brothers and sisters.
Amen.

✍ *The prayer is based on: Jn 11[52] / Gen 1[27], Wis 2[23] / Lk 1[48], Jn 15[15] / Lk 24[31] / 1 Pet 3[8], 1 Jn 4[20]*

"Set free the captives" - Isaiah 61 & Lk 4[16-22]

✍ *In 1996, 83-year old Mrs Rosa Parkes was awarded the Presidential medal of Freedom by President Clinton.*

♪ Amazing grace; God's Spirit is in my heart; O Lord, all the world belongs to you.

1   The Chinese New Year falls between mid-January and late-February. The celebrations last for two weeks. On houses during this time will be seen coloured lanterns, brightly coloured banners with new year greetings, and arrangements of flowers. Fireworks, a Chinese invention, are let off on the Chinese New Year's Eve. New clothes are worn to mark the end of the old year, casting aside whatever misfortunes there were in the old year.

2   In public, lines of people dance with a long dragon's costume over their heads. The dragon's dance, performed to the accompaniment of drums and gongs, is believed to ward off evil spirits for the year ahead. The New Year celebrations end when children parade through the streets carrying coloured lanterns that they have lit.

3   *For our prayer today we will use words that are based on an ancient Chinese blessing:*

4   **May God guard us and keep us
in safety and comfort
and in health and strength,
sending us nothing but good.
May God send down
so many blessings
that the day is not long enough
for them all.
Amen.**

The date of the Chinese New Year varies in the solar year that we use because it is based on the lunar calendar. In the Chinese communities in Britain, many at this time will use the Cantonese greeting, "Kung hay fat choy", which means, "May you prosper". Each year in the Chinese Calendar is associated with one of twelve animals. With New Year starting in the corresponding months of January/February, the years are named as follows:

*1998 - Tiger
1999 - Rabbit
2000 - Dragon
2001 - Snake
2002 - Horse
2003 - Goat or sheep
2004 - Monkey
2005 - Chicken or rooster
2006 - Dog
2007 - Pig
2008 - Rat
2009 - Ox*

The Chinese believe in a god of the kitchen. Before New Year, the kitchen is cleaned thoroughly. A new paper picture of the 'Kitchen God' is placed behind the stove, where an incense stick will be burned each day. A new picture of the 'Guardian of the Gates' is put up by the door.

The blessing is based on part of the Shi Ching from the Confucian Book of Odes.

May the blessing of God be upon you; Oh the love of my Lord; Sing to the mountains; This day God gives me; This is the day; This, then, is my prayer.

1   Having defeated Napoleon in 1815 at the Battle of Waterloo, it was on this day in 1827, that the Duke of Wellington was appointed Commander-in-Chief of the British Army.

2   After defeating Napoleon, Wellington heard someone say that war was glorious. His reply was:

"Take my word for it:
if you had seen but one day of war,
you would pray to Almighty God
that you might never see such again."

3   On one occasion a deserter from the army was brought before him. Wellington was about to pronounce the death sentence on him, and said:

"I am extremely sorry
to pass this severe sentence,
but we have tried everything,
and all the discipline and penalties
have failed to improve this man
who is otherwise a brave and good soldier."

4   Then the Duke of Wellington invited his fellow-soldiers to speak on his behalf. One of them said:

"Sir, there is one thing you have not tried.
You have not tried forgiving him."

Wellington was struck by these words and told the deserter that he was forgiven. Never again did the soldier desert, and he always showed his appreciation to the Duke.

5. *Let's pray in silence for a moment for someone whom I need to forgive, or for someone who has forgiven me...*

(pause)

6. *Let us pray:*

Father,
I ask you
to help me to be generous
when I think
of the attitude and actions of others.
Forgiving someone
isn't an easy option,
and I know that forgiveness
isn't somehow pretending
that something wrong
hasn't happened.
For what I have done wrong,
forgive me Father,
to the extent
that I am generous in forgiving -
or hoping to forgive -
those who have done wrong to me.
Amen.

 Arthur Wellesley, Duke of Wellington, 1/5/1769 - 14/9/1852

God forgave my sin; Lay your hands; The light of Christ.

(See also 25 January)

1 Today sees the start of the Week of Prayer for Christian Unity.

2 Pope John XXIII *(the twenty-third)* was Pope in the early 1960s and he did a lot for world peace at the time of the Cuban Missile Crisis that almost became World War III. He is also well-known for being very keen to bring closer together Christians of different churches. He said:

> *"In essential things - unity;*
> *in unimportant things - freedom;*
> *in all things - charity."*

3 The end of Church Unity Week on the 25th is the anniversary (in 1959) of the announcement by Pope John that he would call together all the Catholic bishops across the world to look at bringing the Church up-to-date, *"to let in some air and blow away the dust".* That meeting would be called "The Second Vatican Council".

4 Pope John wrote a prayer which we will make our own today:

"Renew in our own days
your miracles
like a second Pentecost.
Grant that the Church,
re-united in prayer,
may extend the kingdom of Jesus
- a kingdom of truth and justice,
of love and peace.
Amen."

📖 *The Cuban missile crisis occurred in 1962.*

📖 *Pope John XXIII [the 23rd] : 25/11/1881-30/6/1963. How significant was his role in world peace can be illustrated from an account of the regard that Soviet Chairman Khrushchev had for Pope John. A medal from the Pope had been given to Khrushchev, and he kept it on his desk in the Kremlin. Whenever Communist party leaders were speaking, Khrushchev would play ostentatiously with the medal, expecting to be asked what it was. He would always reply: "It's a medal from the Pope."*

🎵 Abba, Father, you are the potter; Be still and know I am with you; For I'm building a people of power; Lay your hands; Lord, make me a means of your peace; Make me a channel of your peace; O Lord all the world.

1 Christopher Nolan, a disabled writer, won the Whitbread Book of the Year Award on this day in 1988. He was aged 22. We'll hear some words from his autobiography, in which he talks of recognising the face of God in human form.

2 *"Such were his teachers,*
and such was their imagination,
that the mute boy became constantly amazed
at the almost telepathic degree of certainty
with which they read his facial expression,
eye movements and body language.
Many a good laugh was had
by teacher and pupil
as they deciphered his code.
It was at moments such as these
that Joseph
recognised the face of God
in human form.
It glimmered in their kindness to him,
it glowed in their keenness,
it hinted in their caring;
indeed, it caressed in their gaze."

3 Let's pause to think for a moment of individuals who have been very special for us, in whom we have *"recognised the face of God in human form"*.

   (pause)

4 *Let's pray for our school community*
that, students and teachers together,
we may learn to recognise the face of
God in others today.

   Father,
   teach us to recognise your face
   in the people
   you put into our lives today.
   Amen.

📖 *The quote is from Christopher Nolan's 'Under the Eye of the Clock', published by Weidenfeld and Nicolson Ltd, London, 1987, page 11.*

📖 *Recognising Jesus walking beside us [Emmaus] - Luke 24$^{13\text{-}35}$.*

🎵 Father, in my life I see; Father I place into your hands; If I am lacking love.

20 JANUARY

(See also 12 May)

1 When a General Election in Britain produces a new Prime Minister, he or she takes over the government on that very day.

2 In the United States, a new President does not take up office until the 20th January, known as "Inauguration Day".

3 This day in 1961 was the Inauguration Day of the 43-year old President, John F Kennedy. In his inaugural speech, he reflected on personal responsibility when he said:

4 *"Ask not what your country*
   can do for you.
   Ask what you can do
   for your country."

5 Whilst each of us has rights, we also have responsibilities towards others.

6 *Let us pray:*

God our Father,
  with the gifts you have given to us
  we have responsibilities and duties.
Inspire us to take the initiative
  in treating others
  as we would like them to treat us.
Amen.

🖙 *An alternative prayer is that of 26 April or 12 May.*

🖙 *Micah 6^8 - Act justly, love tenderly, and walk humbly with your God.*

♪ God's Spirit is in my heart; Happy the man; If I am lacking love; I give my hands; O Lord all the world; Take my hands.

(See also 22 January)

1 Queen Victoria, after the death of her husband (Prince Albert), spent a good part of her time at Balmoral Castle in the Scottish Highlands. Walking one day by herself, it started to rain. Queen Victoria stopped for shelter at a nearby cottage, and knocked on the door, hoping to be able to borrow an umbrella.

2 The woman inside did not recognise the Queen, and the Queen didn't say who she was. The woman showed her annoyance at being disturbed. She closed her door, with the Queen still standing outside, and then chose a broken umbrella to lend her. *"Here"*, she said in a nasty way, as she thrust it into the hands of the Queen, quickly closing the door on her again. Having thanked her, Queen Victoria returned to Balmoral Castle.

3 The following morning, several of the Queen's men drove to the cottage in full uniform. *"Madam, the Queen thanks you and returns the umbrella that you lent to her."* The woman was annoyed and ashamed when she realised it was the Queen to whom she had been nasty and short-tempered to. The men heard her mutter:

"If only I'd known,
I'd have given her my best umbrella."

4 *Let us pray:*

Lord,
inspire me to live in such a way
that I always give of my best
and be welcoming and generous
towards others. Amen.

5 | *"If only I'd known, I'd have given my best."* |

✍ *Matthew 25³¹⁻⁴⁶ - those who live in such a way that goodness is second-nature to them; they don't realise that it is Jesus whom they are helping: they help simply because someone needs help.*

✍ *Balmoral Castle is about 65km [45 miles] west of Aberdeen.*

✍ *Aged 11, and realising that she would someday become Queen, Victoria spoke of how she would act as Queen: "I will be good", she said. She became Queen 7 years later.*

✍ *See also 29 May about doing my best.*

♪ All that I am; Do not worry over what to eat ("go do your best today"); Take my hands; Whatsoever you do.

22 JANUARY

(See also 21 January and 29 April)

1 The ship called *"The Queen Mary"* was one of the finest of British ships. Shortly before the ship's launch in 1934, Sir Thomas Royden, one of the directors of the shipping company, Cunard, met King George V *(the 5th)*, intending to ask his permission to name the new ship *"The Queen Victoria".*

2 Royden asked the king if the ship could be named *"after the greatest queen this country has ever known."* King George, presuming the words were being said of his wife (Queen Mary), said: *"That is the greatest compliment ever paid to my wife. I'll ask her if your ship may be named after her."* It was only years later that the shipping company mentioned that it had been intending to call the ship *"The Queen Victoria"* !

3 Queen Victoria herself died on this day in 1901.

4 There is always a great ceremony when ships are named, and a bottle is broken on the bow of the ship. We celebrate when people are given their name at the time of baptism (christening).

5 If someone is not bothered to call people by their name, it might reflect a lack of care and respect. We know that Adolf Hitler's father never called him by his name, but whistled for him (like for a dog) whenever he wanted him. In some countries, prisoners are called by numbers rather than by their names as a way of de-humanising them, of taking away their individuality.

6 Let's think in silence for a moment of one person whom I could value and respect more. In what specific ways can I show respect and appreciation to that person today? *(pause)*

7 *Let us pray:*

God our Father,
you call each of us by name,
and you treasure each of us
individually
as though no-one else exists.
Inspire us
to respect and value
each person
who comes into our lives this day.
Amen.

📖 *Victoria was born on 24/5/1819. She became Queen on 20/6/1837, aged 18, and married Prince Albert in 1840. She died on 22/1/1901, having been the longest reigning British monarch - reigning for 63 years. Queen Victoria has been called "The Grandmother of Europe" because her descendants married into all the royal families of Europe, producing heirs who ruled many countries.*

📖 *See 30 April regarding the influences on and the prejudices of Adolf Hitler.*

🎼 Be not afraid; Do not be afraid; I heard the Lord call my name; Oh the word of my Lord.

(See also 4 June)

1   Tomorrow, 24th January is the anniversary of the death of Sir Winston Churchill in 1965. He had given inspiring and courageous leadership to Britain and the Free World - opposing Nazi Germany, Italy and Japan - during the Second World War.

2   Churchill wrote this about how a great nation should act in war and in peace:

> *"In war, resolution;*
> *in defeat, defiance;*
> *in victory, magnanimity;*
> *in peace, goodwill."*

3.   *Let us pray:*

Lord, whilst I pray
for peace and goodwill in our world,
I ask you to help me
to change my own attitude
for the better,
so that peace and goodwill
may start with the way I behave
towards those who have hurt me.
Inspire me to be as generous to others
as I would like them to be with me.
Amen.

📖 *"Magnanimity" - generosity [this word could replace "magnanimity" if the passage above is read aloud]: more generous and merciful than might be expected, especially if the victor has suffered.*

📖 *On his 75th birthday, Churchill said: "I am ready to meet my Maker. Whether my Maker is ready for the ordeal of meeting me is another matter!"*

🎵   Lord, make me a means of your peace;
Make me a channel of your peace.

24 JANUARY

1 Between 1984 and 1992, men from Europe and the United States were taken as hostages in Beirut, the capital of the Lebanon.

2 Terry Waite, a special envoy of the Archbishop of Canterbury, helped negotiate the release of four Britons. He was on his fifth trip to Beirut to negotiate the freedom of other hostages when he was taken captive himself.

3 He was kept in complete isolation for four years. Like the other hostages, there were no windows or fresh air in his small cell, and he was chained to a wall, sometimes weeks without any light. He suffered cruelty and torture, and became very ill. It would be 1,763 days before he would be released.

4 Terry Waite tells of a postcard from Britain that somehow reached him, and which his guards surprisingly passed on to him. The postcard - from someone he didn't know - read:

5 *"Dear Terry.*
You are not forgotten. People everywhere are praying for your release, and that of other hostages.
With best wishes,
Joy Brodier.

6 On his release in November 1991, Terry praised the work of agencies like Amnesty International with their letter-writing campaigns, supporting prisoners of conscience: letters written to prisoners of conscience themselves, and courteous letters to their captors or governments.

7 *Let's pray in silence for a moment for people across the world, like Terry Waite, who are prisoners of conscience...*

✍ *Could use as a prayer that of 24 March*

✍ *The quote from the postcard is taken from "Taken on Trust", Terry Waite's inspiring autobiography: Hodder and Stoughton, page 263; ISBN 0-340-58196-4.*

✍ *The picture on the postcard was of John Bunyan, the writer of "Pilgrim's Progress", in his prison cell - a prisoner of conscience as a Non-Conformist [in his case, a Puritan] in Anglican England. He was imprisoned in Bedford County Jail from 1660-1672.*

✍ *In 1961 the Quakers founded 'Amnesty International' for the support of prisoners of conscience throughout the world. The symbol of Amnesty International is a lit candle surrounded by barbed wire - hope amidst unjust imprisonment. Amnesty International, 1 Easton Street, London WC1X 8DJ. They can supply names and details of prisoners of conscience, suggesting writing to the prisoner and to that country's government. See also 5 March regarding the Quakers.*

♪ God's Spirit is in my heart; He who would valiant be (written by John Bunyan); Lord of all hopefulness.

JANUARY 25

(See also 26/27 January)

1 Those who have been on holiday to Malta, may know that one of the bays is called Saint Paul's Bay, in the north of the island. It bears that name because Saint Paul was shipwrecked there on his way to prison in Rome.

2 Today is the Feast of the Conversion of Saint Paul. Originally he was known as "Saul", a Jewish leader who worked hard for the total destruction of the Christian Church, going from house to house to arrest people and put them in prison. This persecution was taking place after the Resurrection of Jesus, as more and more people became Christians.

3 On a journey to Damascus, though, Saul was struck blind by a bright light suddenly shining around him. He fell to the ground and heard a voice: *"Saul, Saul, why are you persecuting me?"* Saul asked: *"Who are you?"* The voice replied: *"I am Jesus of Nazareth, and you are persecuting me."*

4 Saul asked: *"What am I to do, Lord?"* The voice replied: *"Stand up and go into Damascus. There you will be told what to do."*

5 Blind as he now was, Saul's companions had to lead him by the hand into Damascus. After three days, a man called Ananias had a vision, telling him to visit the blind Saul. At first he resisted, knowing that Saul had set out to imprison Christians, not to become one of them! He wondered if this was a trap, but the Lord told him: *"You must go all the same, because Saul is the one I have chosen to bring the Gospel to many people."*

6 And so Ananias visited Saul and said to him: *"Saul, I have been sent by the Lord Jesus who appeared to you on your jour-* *ney here. Be filled with the Holy Spirit, and receive back your sight."* Saul's sight was restored, and he was baptised a Christian.

7 From having persecuted Christians, he himself followed Christ and helped to spread the Gospel throughout various parts of the world.

8 *Let us pray, using some words of blessing that Paul wrote to the Christians in Corinth:*

May the life of the Lord Jesus, and the love of God the Father, and the companionship of the Holy Spirit be with us all. Amen. *(2 Cor 13[13])*

📖 *Today, the Feast of the Conversion of Saint Paul, marks the end of Christian Unity week.*

📖 *The conversion of Saul, becoming Paul - Acts of the Apostles, 8[1.3], 9[1-30], and also 22[3-16] Paul's shipwreck on Malta on the way to Rome - Acts 27[1]-28[11]*

📖 *Malta is in the Mediterranean, near the large island of Sicily which is south of Italy. The area of the largest island of Malta is 246 sq km [95 sq miles]. During the Second World War, the island of Malta was awarded the George Cross by King George VI, in recognition of the people's courage against the bombers of Mussolini's Italy and Hitler's Germany.*

🎵 Abba Father, you are the potter; Amazing grace; Be still and know I am with you; For I'm building a people of power; Here I am; Lay your hands; O Lord all the world; This then is my prayer.

26 JANUARY

(See also 25/27 January)

1 Yesterday was the Feast of the Conversion of Saint Paul. We're going to listen to some words that Paul wrote to the Christians living in Rome, and we'll use his words to reflect and pray today:

2 *Do not let your love be a sham,*
but be sincere
in choosing good rather than evil.
Have warm affection for one another
as Christian brothers and sisters.

3 *Be committed and enthusiastic*
as you work for the Lord,
being happy and cheerful
as you place your trust in him.
Live in God's presence
and keep on praying.
When difficulties arise, be patient.
Set out to welcome others
and be generous with those in need.
Don't curse others; bless them,
even when they
have not been good to you.
Do all you can to live in peace
with everyone.

4 *Support and encourage others*
by rejoicing with those who are happy,
and sharing the sadness
of those who are in sorrow.
Never look down on another person,
but always be positive
in your attitude to others.
Be as concerned
for those who can do nothing for you
in return
as for those who are very close to you.
Break the cycle of evil
- conquer it with goodness.

(Romans 12$^{9-18,21}$)

Christ is our king; Do not worry; Follow me; If I am lacking love; If God is for us *(text = Paul to the Romans - same text as 'For to those who love God')*; I give my hands.

(See also 25/26 January)

1   In the New Testament there are 27 short books. We have the 4 gospels, then the "Acts of the Apostles", telling of the actions of the first Christians after the resurrection of Jesus. The last book of the Bible is called "Revelation" or "Apocalypse". The rest of the New Testament is a collection of 21 letters - 13 of them were written by Saint Paul.

2   Paul is mentioned often in the "Acts of the Apostles". We can read this short passage, for example, in which we find a word repeated:

3   *"Paul sent for the disciples.*
He spoke words of encouragement to them,
said goodbye,
and then set off for Macedonia.
He gave much encouragement
to the people he met on his journey,
and then made his way into Greece."

(Acts 20$^{1-2}$)

4   The word that appears twice is *"encouragement"*. Let's pause for a moment to focus on one person whom I can set out to encourage today, thinking of specific ways in which I can encourage that person.

(pause...)

5   *Let us pray:*

Lord, we ask you to inspire us
to encourage others
by what we say and do today.
Amen.

✍ *The Acts of the Apostles was written by St Luke - see how the opening paragraph of 'Luke's Gospel' matches up with the first sentence of 'the Acts of the Apostles'.*

✍ *In his writings, Paul refers to himself as an "apostle" (e.g Rom 1^1, 2 Cor 1^1), but he was not one of what we call "the 12 apostles". As we have read, Paul never met Jesus before his death and resurrection. The word "apostle" means "messenger", whilst "disciple" means "one who learns, a student".*

✍ *Mark Twain: "I can live for 6 months on a compliment".*

♪   If I am lacking love; Oh the word of my Lord.

28 JANUARY

1 On this day in 1986 the United States' Space Shuttle "Challenger" roared into the sky from Cape Canaveral in Florida. The world's TV cameras were focused on the rocket as it carried five men and two women. One of the women, Christa McAuliffe (a high school teacher), had won a contest to be the first "ordinary person" in space.

2 Millions of people watched live on television as, suddenly, a minute after blast-off, "Challenger" exploded.

3 In a speech to the people of the United States, President Ronald Reagan quoted a few lines from a poem written by a 19-year old British Second World War pilot, John Magee, who was killed in an air-collision in 1941 just three months after writing the poem. John Magee captures something of the spirit and adventure of flying, and talks of having put out his hand and touched the face of God. We'll use his poem to reflect and pray today:

4 *Oh! I have slipped the surly bonds of Earth*
And danced the skies
    on laughter-silvered wings;
Sunward I've climbed,
    and joined the tumbling mirth
Of sun-split clouds - and done a hundred
    things
You have not dreamed of
    - wheeled and soared and swung
High in the sunlit silence. Hov'ring there,
I've chased the shouting wind along.
    and flung
My eager craft through footless halls of air.
Up, up the long, delirious burning blue
I've topped the wind-swept heights
    with easy grace,
Where never lark, or even eagle flew -
And, while with silent, lifting mind I've trod
The high untrespassed sanctity of space,
Put out my hand and touched the face of God.

📖 *In a nationwide poll in 1995 of Britain's favourite poetry, this poem came 43rd. The last few lines of the poem are quoted in the moving film, "The man without a face" (1993) starring Mel Gibson.*

🎶 Oh Lord my God, the Father of creation; O Lord my God, when I in awesome wonder; On eagle's wings *(being a setting of Psalm 91/90).*

JANUARY 29

(See also 30 January, 12 May)

1 Mohandas Gandhi was born in India in 1869. He spent 3 years in Britain, training to be a lawyer, and then lived for 21 years in South Africa, where he saw and experienced much racial prejudice and discrimination. Gandhi encouraged some of the Indian workers in South Africa to go on strike and march in a non-violent way. The government responded with violence, killing many.

2 Gandhi left South Africa in 1915, after the government made some important concessions for a more just treatment of non-whites. He returned to India, where he became known as "Mahatma" (which means "Great Soul") as he began to campaign to make India independent from British rule.

3 He knew that violence was evil, and he also knew that attempts for reasoned discussion often got nowhere. The alternative way was his method of passive, non-violent resistance. His method of non-co-operation included boycotting British goods. At the same time, he also sought to show the Indian people that they needed to remove prejudices and injustices amongst themselves - such as considering some people to be "untouchables", the lowest "caste" of people in India.

4 Gandhi said:

"If you don't find God in the very next person you meet, it is a waste of time looking for him further."

5 Let us pray:

God and Father of all people, never let me look down on others or make anyone feel inferior.

**Show me how to remove any prejudices so that
I may appreciate individuals more for who they are.
Inspire me to live in such a way that I may discover you
. in the people I will meet today.
Amen.**

6 Gandhi said:

"If you don't find God in the very next person you meet, it is a waste of time looking for him further."

🖾 *"Prejudice" is the attitude; "discrimination" is the action.*

🖾 *David Attenborough's outstanding film, 'Gandhi'.*

🖾 *Mohandas [Mahatma] Gandhi: 2/10/1869 - 30/1/1948.*

🎵 Come let us go up to the Lord; Father I place into your hands; If I am lacking love; I give my hands; There is a world.

47

30 JANUARY

(See also 29, 30 January, 17 February, 12 May)

1 In India, Gandhi mounted a campaign of "civil disobedience" against British rule. In 1930, he campaigned against the British tax on salt, which was particularly unfair to the very poor. He marched 600 km (375 miles) to the coast, with many joining him on the way. There he set some sea-water to evaporate in the sun, leaving the salt behind. Paying no tax on the salt, he was put into prison.

2 The Indian "sub-continent" had a sixth of the world's population. Against Gandhi's wishes, different religious groups insisted that the country be partitioned at the time that Independence was granted in 1947. Pakistan was to be of mainly Muslim people, and the remaining part (to be called "India") of mainly Hindus and Sikhs. Up to ten million people began to move, thinking they would be persecuted in a country of a different religion. There was terrible bloodshed as Hindus, Sikhs and Muslims turned on one another, and about 220,000 people were killed. Gandhi announced that he would fast - would go without food - even if that would result in his death, unless the people stopped fighting and killing one another. He was successful.

3 It was on this day, 30th January, in 1948, as Gandhi was walking to a prayer meeting, that a fellow-Hindu killed Gandhi with a shot from a gun. So shocked was everyone by Gandhi's murder, that the communal violence that had started up again came to an end.

4 Gandhi and his followers had fought prejudice and discrimination with courage, informing people of the truth, and practising non-violence. Gandhi set out to look at matters from the viewpoint of those who thought differently from himself.

5 He advised people to say to themselves each morning:
*"I shall not fear anyone.
I shall not bear ill-feelings
toward anyone."*

6 *Let us pray:*

Lord,
   this day and forever,
   may I have the courage
   never to be afraid of anyone.
May I have the generosity
   to bear ill-feeling toward no-one.
Lead me to live in such a way
   as to treat others
   in the same way
   as I would like to be treated.
Inspire me
   never to be violent
   in thought, word or action,
   and lead me
   to conquer evil with goodness.
Amen.

7 *"I shall not fear anyone.
I shall not bear ill-feelings toward
anyone."*

📖 *Gandhi also said:*
"No sacrifice is worth the name unless it is a joy. Sacrifice and a long face go ill together."

📖 *In 1971, East Pakistan declared independence from West Pakistan, and the East is now called Bangladesh.*

📖 *Martin Luther King - see 15 January, 4/5 April - followed Gandhi's practice of non-violence.*

🎼 All that I am; If I am lacking love; Lord, make me a means; Make me a channel; O Lord all the world; There is a world; This is what Yahweh asks of you.

1 Today is the feastday of Saint John Bosco, who was born in Turin, northern Italy. Of a very poor family himself, he knew what poor and unemployed people were going through. Some 400 boys (many of them orphans and street children) gathered round Father John Bosco, and he begged money to educate them and give them somewhere to live. So that the boys could get a job, he set up workshops. Some were then able to become apprentices in making shoes and clothes, and others gained work experience with a printing press that John had set-up.

2 He learned acrobatics and magic tricks which appealed to the boys. He accompanied groups of young people on country walks, picnics and games, and he ended everything with prayer.

3 John Bosco said:

"Young people should not only be loved
but they must know
that they are loved."

4 *Let us pray:*

Lord, show me how to live today
  with genuine concern for others.
In expressing my care,
  may I show people
  that they are valued,
  loved and appreciated
  for who they are.
Amen.

📖 *John Bosco: 1815-1888. He founded a religious order of men, the Salesians, and also helped to found an order of sisters who would carry out similar work with girls.*

🎵 Here I am, Lord; If I am lacking love; I give my hands; I will be with you; O let all who thirst; Take my hands.

1 The Greek philosopher, Socrates, was sitting by the roadside one day, when he was approached by a traveller who was making his way towards Athens.

2 The traveller asked:
"What sort of people live in Athens?"
So Socrates asked him:
"What sort of people live in *your* own town?"
"Awful," the traveller said. "They are horrible, lying layabouts."

3 And Socrates replied:
"I am *sorry* to tell you that you will find the people of Athens to be just the same as you have found your own people."

4 Soon another traveller came by, who also asked:
"What sort of people live in Athens?"
And Socrates asked him:
"What sort of people live in *your* own town?"
"Marvellous people," the second traveller said; "kind, generous, friendly, honest people."

5 Socrates smiled and said:
"I am *pleased* to tell you that you will find the people of Athens to be just the same as you have found your own people!"

6 *(Pause...)*

7 *And so we pray:*

Lord, we come before you as we are.
We ask you to take away from us
    all that makes us less than human.
Strengthen us
    with the power of your Spirit
    that our attitude and outlook
    may develop,
    and our "way of looking"
    may become more like yours.

Help us to remain positive -
    encouraging and appreciating
    one another,
    looking upon people
    in the same way that you do.
Amen.

❖-❖-❖-❖-❖-❖-❖-❖-❖-❖-❖-❖-❖-❖-❖-❖

 *An alternative prayer would be that of 18 February*

 *"pre-judging" = "prejudice"*

 *Let each of us think about the attitude we have: Sometimes we label and judge people before we've even met them.*

Sometimes we look for things to complain about and we are negative in what we think and say.

Sometimes we think the worst of people and situations. Some of us say we believe people are equal, but then act in a superior way, looking down on those we might think are different.

 If I am lacking love

2 FEBRUARY

A candle may be lit.

1. Today is 40 days after Christmas Day. The feast is called "Candlemas" or "The Presentation of the Lord".

2. It was 40 days after the birth of Jesus that his parents presented him to God the Father in the Temple in Jerusalem. At his Presentation in the Temple, Jesus was recognised for who he was by two people - Simeon and Anna. They were elderly and had spent their lives growing closer to God. Now they meet him face to face and recognise him in their midst.

3. Simeon prays: *"Now, Master, you can let your servant die in peace because my eyes have seen your salvation which you have prepared for all nations to see. He will be a light to enlighten all people."*

4. Because Simeon referred to Jesus as the one who brings light to all nations, candles are lit this day, and the feastday is often called "Candlemas".

5. *The response to our prayers will be: May your light be reflected in us.*

   May your light be reflected in us.

6. Lord Jesus, 40 days after your birth
   you were taken to the Temple
   and presented by your parents
   to God our Father.
   Make us aware that we are the Temple
   of your Holy Spirit who lives in us.

   May your light be reflected in us.

7. Simeon's eyesight grew dim,
   but he recognised who you were.
   Open our eyes
      that we may always recognise you
      in our midst.

   May your light be reflected in us.

8. Simeon prophesied
   that Mary would be pierced
   to the heart.
   As Mary stayed with Jesus
   in his suffering,
   we pray that we may help
   those who are part of our lives.

   May your light be reflected in us.

9. You said
   that you are the light of the world.

   May your light be reflected in us.

📖 *Luke 2²²⁻⁴⁰:the Presentation in the Temple; Jn 8¹² - I am the light of the world; Mt 5¹⁴⁻¹⁶ - you are the light of the world; Lk 8¹⁶⁻¹⁸ & 11³³⁻³⁶ - parable of the lamp;*

📖 The word "gentiles" in Luke 2 means "non-Jews"

🎵 Be still and know I am with you; The light of Christ; Walk in the light

1 Power companies that generate electricity look in advance at the timing of TV programmes. If millions of people watch the same programme and then switch on their kettles, there can be a huge power surge throughout the country's National Electricity Grid. If the power companies are not ready in advance to produce extra electricity, fuses will blow, cutting off electricity to various parts of the country. So it is essential that they look ahead to the timing of TV programmes.

2 At Christmas 1996 the BBC showed the final episode of the comedy 'Only Fools and Horses'. With over 22 million people watching that programme, the year's greatest power surge was triggered as millions switched on their electric kettles at the same time as the programme finished.

3 *Let's pray for the gift*
of being able to see what is needed:

Lord, there are times
when we are so concerned
about ourselves
that we don't think of others.
We ask for the gift of your Spirit
that we may grow in awareness
of others:

4 **- noticing when someone is unhappy,**
- sensing when there's something
wrong for somebody,
- seeing when someone feels cut off
or isolated,
- knowing when to say the right word,
- expressing thanks and compliments,
- being thoughtful when someone is ill,
- giving words of encouragement,
- helping someone to feel welcome,
- realising when someone needs the
opportunity to talk.
May we grow in sensitivity
towards others. Amen.

 If I am lacking love

53

4 FEBRUARY

1 This was the birthday in Germany in 1906 of Dietrich Bonhoeffer. He became a minister in the Lutheran Church and was outspoken about what was wrong when the Nazis first came to power. He spent two years as a minister in a church in London, but chose to return to Germany once it became clear that war would break out. He wrote, *"I will have no right to be a part of the reconstruction of Germany after the war if I do not share in this time with my people."* Like many others, he must have had great courage, intending to do whatever he could to oppose the evil being done in the name of his country. He knew the risks for himself in remaining a critic of the Nazi government and, on his return to Germany, every move of his was watched.

2 In July 1944 a plot to kill Hitler failed. Bonhoeffer was one of many who was implicated in that threat, and he was imprisoned. Less than a month before Germany's surrender he was taken into the prison yard and hanged, aged 39. The prison doctor said of his death: *"I saw Pastor Bonhoeffer kneeling on the floor in prayer. I was most deeply moved by the way this lovable man prayed, so certain that God heard his prayer."*

3 Dietrich wrote this short prayer about love and hatred, and we can make the prayer our own today by thinking of those people with whom we haven't got on very well over the years:

4 **"Lord God,
give me such love
for you and for others
that it will blot out
all hatred and bitterness."**

❖❖❖❖❖❖❖❖❖❖❖❖❖❖❖❖❖❖❖❖

📖 *Was it right to support a plot to overthrow Hitler? To overthrow other governments? Can that be reconciled with "Do not kill" and 1 Peter 2^{13-17}: respect for the civil authorities?*

📖 *Dietrich Bonhoeffer wrote: "We must learn to regard people less in the light of what they do or omit to do, and more in the light of what they suffer."*

God forgave my sin; He who would valiant be; Lord, make me a means; Oh the love of my Lord

1 Henry Thoreau is best remembered as a philosopher - one who explores the meaning of life and the values to live by. He was from the United States. In the mid-1800s he made a decision to be prepared to go to jail for refusing to pay a tax which went to support a war with Mexico. It was his view that the war with Mexico was a means of extending slavery further south. A friend of Thoreau (another philosopher and writer), Ralph Waldo Emerson (who also hated slavery) visited him in jail, saying:
"Henry, why are you here in jail?"
Thoreau replied,
"Why are you <u>not</u> here in jail?"

2 Thoreau wrote:
"Under a government
which imprisons anyone unjustly,
the true place for a just person
is in prison."

3 Thoreau discussed and wrote about *"passive resistance"*, a method of protest that the Indian leader Gandhi later adopted against British rule in his country. *"Passive resistance"* was also used by civil rights activists (such as Martin Luther King in the USA) in the 1960s.

4 *Let us pray in the words of Saint Ignatius:*

Teach us, good Lord,
to give and not to count the cost;
to fight and not to heed the wounds;
to toil and not to seek for rest;
to labour and to ask for no reward,
save that of knowing
that we do your will.
Amen.

🖎 *Conscientious objectors; standing by principles; prisoners of conscience; refusing to pay some taxes; passive resistance; origin of slavery in the USA.*

🖎 *Henry David Thoreau: 12/7/1817-6/5/1862. He said:*
"If a man believes and expects great things of himself, it makes no difference where you put him. He will be surrounded by grandeur."

 He sent me to give; He who would valiant be; Lord, make me a means; Make me a channel; This is what Yahweh asks

6 FEBRUARY

1 In 1958, Manchester United's manager, Matt Busby, had built up such a fine team of young players that they were often called the "Busby Babes".

2 The team had been playing Red Star Belgrade in Yugoslavia and had drawn with them, qualifying for the semi-finals of the European Cup. As the United team were about to fly back home on 6th February, their plane crashed in bad weather on its second attempt to take off from Munich Airport in what was then West Germany. 21 passengers were killed, including 8 of the Manchester United Team. Matt Busby himself was very seriously injured.

3 As it is traditional to have a moment's silence at football matches whenever there has been a disaster, let us pray in silence for a moment - for ourselves and for those we know who have suffered tragedies in their lives. We pray for those who are hurt and wounded because of the splitting up of their family, a death, difficulties with someone, failure, betrayal, the loss of friends, or a serious illness. Let us pray in silence, then, for all who suffer in their lives...

(pause ...)

📧 *Other national tragedies e.g. Aberfan, Bradford, Dunblane, Hillsborough, Hungerford, Kings Cross.*

 Abide with me

1 Beside the head of the Queen on British coins appear the letters "F.D.". They are an abbreviation in Latin for the words "Defender of the Faith." This was a title given by the Pope to King Henry VIII, (the eighth) recalling how, in his first years as king, Henry had written a book about the Sacraments, "defending" what Catholics believe. Some years later he would be executing Catholics.

2 February 7th was the birthday in 1478 of Sir Thomas More, who became a man of great learning, a lawyer, and the father of four children. King Henry VIII valued his friendship, appointing him Lord Chancellor - the main government minister of the time. The king knew that Thomas More was above corruption; he was a person of integrity and honesty at a time when money bought what was thought of as 'justice'.

3 The king wanted to divorce his queen (Catherine of Aragon) and marry Ann Boleyn instead. When the Pope proclaimed that that was wrong, the English parliament passed an Act declaring the king to be "Supreme Head of the Church in England", and Henry decided he could do as he wished in many things. This action also led to the destruction ("Dissolution") of many monasteries and cathedrals in England as the king confiscated and sold their lands and possessions.

4 Thomas More knew that he could not agree with what the king was doing and, even though many bishops supported the actions of the king, Thomas remarked that *"their consciences must speak for them; mine must speak for me."* Thomas still considered himself loyal to the king and, when he was condemned to death, he said:
"I die the King's good servant,
but God's first."

5 *Let us pray:*

God our Father,
　teach us to distinguish clearly
　between right and wrong,
　that we may grow in character
　and develop a true sense of values
　through following Jesus,
　your Son and our Brother.
We pray, too, for all
　who are in positions of leadership
　　in our country
　that they may be inspired
　by the values of the gospel.
We pray that they may live
　as people of integrity and honesty,
　growing in a sense
　of duty and responsibility,
　always being aware of the needy,
　and ready to be of service to others.
Amen.

6 | *"I die the King's good servant,* *but God's first."* |

📖 Prisoners of conscience; conscientious objectors; State v Church; "Defender of the Faith"

📖 *Pope Leo X bestowed the title on King Henry VIII in 1521, after the King had written a pamphlet against Luther's teachings. After Henry's later actions, Pope Paul III withdrew the designation, but in 1544 the same title was given to Henry by Act of Parliament.*

🎵 Be still and know I am with you; Follow me; He who would valiant be

1 Sir Giles Gilbert Scott was aged 22 when he won the competition to be the architect to buid an Anglican Cathedral in Liverpool. He died on this day in 1960. Giles not only designed that very inspiring and huge cathedral (and the very big Battersea Power Station by the River Thames in London) but he also designed the red telephone box, many of which have now been replaced in our streets by British Telecom.

2 We can think of the skills that Scott must have needed for designing both the largest Anglican cathedral in the world, and the small red telephone box.

3 Liverpool now has two magnificent cathedrals. Years ago in Liverpool there used to be rivalry - and even hatred - between Catholics and Protestants. Yet it is interesting that it was a Catholic who designed the Anglican Cathedral, and it was an Anglican who designed the Catholic Cathedral. The road connecting the two great churches is called *"Hope Street"*, and we pray today for real *hope and understanding* between all Christians and between all people of good will.

4 *Let us pray:*

Lord, we ask you to open our eyes
  that we may value and appreciate
    all people,
  recognising what we have in common
  rather than focusing
  on what our differences might be.
Inspire us to distinguish
  between what is important
  and what is not,
  and open our minds and hearts
  that we may always be people
    of good will
  who bring life and joy to others.
Amen.

✍ *In a room off the nave of the huge cathedral that Scott built is one of the relatively small red telephone boxes that he designed, donated by British Telecom.*

✍ *See also 18 January regarding Church Unity.*

♪ For I'm building a people of power;
Peace, perfect peace

1 Yesterday we recalled that Sir Giles Gilbert Scott, a Catholic, had designed Liverpool's Anglican Cathedral. In one of the windows in that cathedral appear the words:

"Remember with thanksgiving all those who by diversity of talents and unity of purpose built this Cathedral to God's glory."

2 Mother Teresa of Calcutta often reminded people that each of us is unique, and each has our own contribution to make. Mother Teresa often said:

"I cannot do what you do,
and you cannot do what I do,
*but **together***
we can do something beautiful for God."

3 Let's pray that each of us makes good use of our talents, and that we set out to work well with others:

4 **Lord, you have enriched our lives**
  in many ways,
  and we remember with thanksgiving
  all who have loved, cared for,
  and supported us over the years.
Show us how best
  to use the time and talents
  you have given each of us,
  and lead us to grow in appreciation
  of the contribution that others make.
May your Spirit empower us
  to work well with others
  and bring out the best
  in those with whom we share our lives.
Amen.

✒ *Mother Teresa: 27/8/10 - 5/9/97*

🎼 For I'm building a people of power;
Peace, perfect peace

1   Jesus promised that when two or three would get together in his name, then he would be with them. Let's take him at his word today, and pause to remember that he is present with us, and looks on us with love...

    (pause...)

2   X-rays were discovered by William Röntgen from Germany, who died on this day in 1923. The discovery of X-rays (seeing deep within people) soon led to great developments in medicine. From that time on, doctors would be able to see what was below the surface of the skin without needing to perform operations to do so.

3   We are going to use for our prayer one of the psalms from the Bible. We reflect on God seeing deep within us, always looking on us with love:

4   *Let us pray:*

> **Lord, lover of life,**
> > **you know the depths**
> > **of my innermost self,**
> > **and you understand me.**
> **You protect me on every side,**
> > **shielding me from all harm.**
> **When you put me together carefully**
> > **in my mother's womb,**
> > **you knew all about me.**
> **I thank you for the wonder of myself**
> > **and I stand in awe**
> > **at all that you have made.**
> **Guide me in your ways.**

(from Psalm 138/9)

📖 Videos and pictures of the child developing in the womb; praying for someone who is in hospital

🎵 Be still and know I am with you; Christ be beside me; Yahweh, I know you are near.

(See also 3 May)

1 Bernadette Soubirous was of a very poor family in Lourdes, a small village at the foothills of the Pyrenees in the south of France. It was on this day in 1858, whilst she and her sisters went to collect brushwood for the house fire, that Bernadette saw the first of 18 visions of a lady. As time went on, it became clear that it was Our Lady who was appearing. During one of the visions, the Mother of Jesus told Bernadette to scrape some earth from the ground. A steady spring of water then flowed, and many of the thousands of people who now visit Lourdes each year bathe in that running water.

2 In the convent that she joined, Bernadette said: *"I am getting on with my job."* She was asked: *"What is your job?"* She replied in a positive way, saying: *"Living as somebody who is ill."* Bernadette prayed:

"Lord, I do not ask that I never be afflicted, but only that you never abandon me in affliction."

3 Today is the feastday of Our Lady of Lourdes, and it is appropriate that this day is also set aside each year as *"The World Day of the Sick".*

4 When Pope John Paul visited Britain in 1982, he said:

"Today I make an urgent plea to this nation. Do not neglect your sick and elderly. Do not turn away from the handicapped and dying.
Do not push them to the margins of society for, if you do, you will fail to understand that they represent an important truth. The sick, the elderly, the handicapped and the dying teach us that weakness
is a creative part of human living, and that suffering can be embraced with no loss of dignity. Without the presence of these people in your midst you might be tempted to think of health, strength and power as the only important values to be pursued in life."

5 *Let us pray:*

Father, we pray that we may live cheerfully and patiently and positively both in sickness and in health.
We bring before you all who are sick and all who care for them...
Bring healing of one kind or another to those we know who are ill, afraid or worried.
We think of those who suffer from constant sickness or weakness and those who never get well.
Father, be with them all, and be with us. Amen.

❖•❖•❖•❖•❖•❖•❖•❖•❖•❖•❖•❖•❖•❖•❖•❖

✍ *The day before, could collect names of relatives and friends who are sick, and include their names in today's prayer*

✍ *Pope John Paul's words were spoken as he celebrated the Sacrament of the Sick in Southwark Cathedral, 28/5/82.*

✍ *See also "The Lourdes Pilgrim - A Prayerbook and Guide" by Oliver Todd [Matthew James Publishing Ltd. ISBN: 1 898366 19 5]*

 As I kneel before you; Hail Mary, full of grace; Holy Virgin, by God's decree; Laudato sii; Lay your hands; Mother of God's living word; Sing of a girl

1 Charles Darwin - who would become famous for his theories of evolution - was born on 12th February in 1809.

2 Aged 22, Darwin joined the British explorer ship, HMS Beagle, on their 5-year voyage around the coasts of South America and to other countries. He was a keen observer of how plant and animal life differed in various parts of the world. He realised that plants and animals can change over many generations, adapting and evolving because of their surroundings.

3 In his *"Theory of Evolution by Natural Selection"*, Charles Darwin says that the young born to any living thing compete for survival against everything around them. He realised (for example) that, at a time of famine, the only leaves not eaten on trees would be high up. Small giraffes would die, but those that were tall enough to reach the leaves would live and would then reproduce, and their young would also be tall. Darwin said that only by adapting to surroundings will species survive.

4 In reading the creation stories at the beginning of the Bible, some people have thought of them as a kind of "diary", but many people read them as inspired "parables" that have deep meanings: emphasising that mankind is blessed and is at the centre of God's attention - so much so that God later chose to become one of us.

5 *Let us pray:*

God our Father, open our eyes
that we may sense the wonder and awe
in the splendour of all your creation -
from the stars
that are large and far away,

to people and the tiniest creatures
near us each day.
Help us to become more aware
of how every living thing is special
and to be treated well.
Lead us to respect and value every person
as unique and important,
made in your image and likeness.
We ask this prayer through Jesus,
who became a human being
because you love our world so much.
Amen.

📖 There are two DIFFERENT creation stories in Genesis: 1^1-2^4 and 2^{4-25}

📖 So much could have gone wrong over millions of years - a different atmosphere, meteorites, climate shifts - that the chances of life "just happening to evolve" to our stage, are billions to one against. Surely God has continued to influence? It has been said that for life on earth to have developed and progressed purely by chance could be compared with throwing materials into the air that just happen to come together as they fall back to earth, in the form of an aeroplane!

📖 Darwin wrote to a friend, speaking of "the extreme difficulty or rather impossibility of conceiving this immense and wonderful universe as the result of blind chance. When thus reflecting, I feel compelled to look at a First Cause, and I deserve to be called a Theist [a believer in God]. But then arises the doubt - can the mind of man, which has, as I fully believe, been developed from a mind as low as that possessed by the lowest animals, be trusted when it draws such grand conclusions?"

📖 See also Psalm 103/104 and Psalm 8 [a version of which is printed for 12 April].

🎵 Morning has broken; Thank you for fathers.

1 Let's pause for a moment to remind ourselves that we are in the presence of God who is always faithful...

(pause...)

2 In 1692 the Scottish highland clans still supported the Catholic King James II who was of Scottish descent. The supporters were called "Jacobites" (as "Jacobus" is the Latin for "James"). King James is generally considered not to have been a good king. He had been deposed by Parliament in London in what is called "The Glorious Revolution", and they invited the Protestant William of Orange to be king in his place.

3 Each Scottish clan had to swear to be loyal to the new king, or they would be imprisoned and have their lands confiscated. The chief of the MacDonald clan signed his oath of loyalty, but was a week late in doing so because blizzards had prevented him from travelling.

4 A hundred soldiers, including some of the Campbell clan (who were long-standing enemies of the MacDonalds) were sheltered and fed in Glencoe by the MacDonalds for over a week. Early one morning, the soldiers turned on the MacDonalds who had given them hospitality, and murdered the chief of the clan and some of the men, women and children. They had received orders to kill the people.

5 Why was this Massacre at Glencoe (one of many in those days) thought to be even worse than murder itself?

6 Those who were taken in as guests turned on those who had looked after them. They murdered those who had given them hospitality. King William's ministers (if not also the king himself)

certainly knew what was going to happen. It was "political murder" as it was meant to be a "lesson" to all who might think of rebelling against the new king.

7 *Let us pray:*

God our Father,
   the Bible reminds us
   that your love for each of us is great
   and that you are faithful for ever,
   never letting us down
   or forgetting your promises to us.
Inspire us to value friendship and loyalty,
   that we may be faithful
   to those who love and trust us.
We pray that we may live in such a way
   that we may make others feel
   welcome and secure.
Show us how
   to look upon other people
   in the same generous way
   that you look upon each of us.
Extend our horizons
   that we may understand better
   those who are far from us.
Amen.

📖 *"Make hospitality your special care" - Romans 12$^{9-13}$. "Welcome strangers; some have welcomed angels" - Hebrews 13$^{1-3}$.*

📖 *Other examples of treachery after hospitality - Jesus' betrayal after the Last Supper [Lk 22^{47} ff]. In 1996, in the light of the terror of Saddam Hussein's rule in Iraq, one of his sons-in-law fled to Jordan with his family. On being invited to return, he was tortured and murdered.*

📖 *William of Orange became King William III.*

🎵 If I am lacking love; Make me a channel; There is a world; Whatsoever you do

14 FEBRUARY

1 We generally think of 14th February as St Valentine's Day. We don't know who Valentine was, but there are many legends about him. One of the stories names him as a bishop when the Roman emperor of the time made it a law that no Roman soldier should be allowed to marry. The emperor thought that his soldiers would not fight well in his many wars if they were afraid to risk dying in battle because of great love for their wives and families.

2 The story tells us that Bishop Valentine said that the emperor's law was not right; it was unjust - men and women have the right to marry and have families. Soldiers began to approach the bishop, and so he arranged marriages secretly. Word got back to the emperor, but Valentine was courageous in speaking before him: *"I have promised to serve God who loves us, and I obey his laws."* According to this legend, Bishop Valentine was put into prison where he died on this day - a patron saint of all who are in love.

3 *Let us pray:*

Father, we read in the Bible
　　that the best way to describe you
　　is to use the word "Love".
Your love for mankind is so great
　　that you sent Jesus, your Son,
　　to live as one of us.
We pray that we may appreciate
　　and value one another.
God of love,
　　lead us to grow in love. Amen.

❖❖❖❖❖❖❖❖❖❖❖❖❖❖❖❖❖❖❖

 Love: John 3^{16}; 1 Cor 13; 1 John 3-4

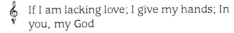 If I am lacking love; I give my hands; In you, my God

1 This was the birthday in 1874 of Ernest Shackleton, who would become an explorer of the South Pole. In the London *'Times'* newspaper, Shackleton printed a small advertisement:

2 *"Men wanted for hazardous journey.*
Small wages, bitter cold,
long months of complete darkness,
constant danger, safe return doubtful.
Honour and recognition
in case of success."

3 5,000 people replied to the advertisement, and Sir Ernest Shackleton selected 27 to join him in his exploration of Antarctica, the South Pole.

4 Let's pause for a moment to think why it might have been that so many replied to that advertisement.

(pause...)

5 *Let us pray:*

God our Father,
there are many difficulties
and challenges in life,
and we see or experience
more of them
each day we live.
Give us the power of your Holy Spirit
that we may have courage and
determination,
and may live in such a way
that we encourage one another.
Enable us to transform
whatever is negative,
and remain positive in attitude
throughout our lives.
Lighten our darkness
and keep us safe. Amen.

📖 *Why were there so many applications for something so hazardous? Maybe people wanted a challenge, an adventure, something exciting, being willing even to risk their lives.*

📖 *Other examples of courage amidst adversity e.g. hostages, astronauts;*

📖 *commitment of Christians in time of persecution*

🎵 Amazing grace; Be still and know I am with you; He who would valiant be

1 Howard Carter, the archaeologist, and his patron, Lord Carnarvon (who gave him money in sponsorship) both researched and dug in the Valley of the Kings in Egypt to find some of the remains of the pharaohs, the rulers of Egypt from about 3000 years before Christ. Carter and Carnarvon hoped that they might find a tomb that had not been looted and its treasures stolen, as had happened to the other tombs and pyramids.

2 One of Howard Carter's workers discovered a set of steps under a pile of rubble. At the bottom of the steps was a sealed door which Carter opened. He had made one of the greatest archaeological discoveries of all time: this was the unopened tomb of Tutankhamen who had become Pharaoh as a young boy in about 1343 B.C., ruling for only nine years before his early death at about the age of 18. Carter was amazed to find its treasures still there - statues, ornaments, furniture, vases and treasure chests.

3 A further door was discovered in that room and, on this day in 1923, the sealed door was opened. Carter peered in. From behind him, a voice was heard: "What do you see?"
   "Wonderful things!" replied Carter.

4 *Let us pray:*

   Lord Jesus,
     as you touched
     the eyes of the blind man,
     touch us
     so that our eyes may be opened
     so that we can "really see"
     the many wonderful things around us
     and in our own lives.
   Amen.

✒ *The Tutankhamen exhibition toured the world*

✒ *Song: "What a wonderful world" by Louis Armstrong*

✒ *Some of the "wonderful things" we tend to take for granted - stars at night; intricacy of a flower; uniqueness of each fingerprint; different kinds of movement of a thumb; everyday miracle of birth; life of a tiny insect*

✒ *What "wonderful things" would each person like to see?*

✒ *See the first paragraph of the book's Introduction for several quotes on "wonder".*

♪ Christ is our king; God's Spirit is in my heart; I give my hands

(See also 29 & 30 January and 12 May)

1 It was under the leadership of Mahatma Gandhi and his practice of "passive resistance" that India achieved her independence from Great Britain in 1947.

2 In his autobiography, Gandhi talks of his days as a student in South Africa, feeling drawn to Jesus and the practice of Christianity. And so he set out one Sunday to go to a Christian church. There, at the entrance to the church, he was told that, if he wanted to attend a service, he must do so in a church reserved for black people, and not in that church building which only white people were allowed to attend. Gandhi no longer felt drawn to Christianity!

3 There is a saying that

*"I might be the only gospel
that others will read today."*

4 *Let us pray:*

**Inspire us, Lord,
to take the gospel more seriously,
that we may be credible witnesses
of your love. Amen.**

 What impression do I leave with others?

God's Spirit is in my heart

18 FEBRUARY

1 In 1564 this day saw the death of Michelangelo Buonarroti, one of the greatest artists, architects and sculptors who ever lived. He was commissioned to paint the ceiling and one of the walls in the Sistine Chapel in the Vatican, Rome (the chapel in which the cardinals gather to elect a new pope). Michelangelo was the architect of part of the massive church of St Peter's, Rome, and he designed its great dome.

2 Michelangelo thought of himself mainly as a sculptor. Two of his most famous pieces of sculpture are 'David' (in Florence) and 'the Pieta' in St Peter's (the dead Jesus in his mother's arms).

3 Michelangelo often saw potential in things that others did not see. On one occasion he was seen to be studying carefully what others simply saw as a large block of marble, and someone asked him just what he was doing. He was looking at the grain of the marble and its strengths, and he said: *"I can see an angel imprisoned in the marble, and I must set it free."* He began the long and skilled job of carving a beautiful angel out of that stone.

4 The story is a reminder that some people only see things as useless; others see beauty and potential.

5 *Let us pray:*

God our Father,
   give us the power of your Spirit
   that we may see and love in others
   what you see and love in them.
We want to see the positive in people
   and bring out the best in each other.
It's easy to say that,
   but not always easy to live it out,
   and so we ask you
   to help and inspire us
   to live as you would like us to live
      this day.
Amen.

1 "CORN FLAKES" first went on sale today in the USA in 1906. Corn flakes are made from "corn on the cob", often called "maize". It is grown in the southern **United States of America.**

2 Some people will have eaten **WEETABIX** for breakfast, produced from the golden wheat grown in **Canada**.

3 The rice in **RICE KRISPIES** is probably grown in **China** or the countries of **south-east Asia**.

4 Some eat **PORRIDGE** - made from oats grown in **Scotland** or East Anglia in **England.**

5 **SUGAR** will have been refined from sugar-beet grown in **East Anglia**, or from sugar-cane grown in the **West Indies**.

6 **MILK** and **EGGS** will have been produced in **Britain**.

7 **BACON** may be **British** or **Irish** or **Danish**.

8 Many of us will have eaten toast today. To make a crisp loaf of **BREAD**, **England's** wheat-flour has to be blended with varieties of wheat grown in the **U.S.A.**

9 **BUTTER** may have come from **Britain, Ireland** or **Denmark**, or from **New Zealand**, one of our Commonwealth partners.

10 **MARMALADE** is often made from the famous Seville oranges of southern **Spain**. **GRAPEFRUIT** or **ORANGE JUICE** may have come from fruit grown in the southern **United States** or from around Jaffa in **Israel**.

11 **TEA** is grown in **India** and in **Sri Lanka**, where tea is generally called "Ceylon" after the former name of the country. **COFFEE** may have been shipped to us from **Kenya** or **Colombia** or **Brazil**.

12 We can see how many people from many different places throughout the world have some influence on our lives.

13 *Let us pray to be appreciative*
of all who influence our lives,
including many whom we will never
meet:

God our Father, I thank you today
   for those people
   whom I will never know
   who make my life better
      for what they offer
      - those far away, and those very near.
More and more
      may I come to appreciate and respect
      everyone who is a part of my life.
Amen.

✍ *A map could be used to indicate these countries, and the appropriate food could be displayed.*

20 FEBRUARY

1   Philosophers think of what life is about and the way we should live. One of the greatest philosophers and teachers died today in 1694. Voltaire was a Frenchman, and he said:

"I do not agree with what you say,
but I would be prepared to die
to defend your right to say it."

2   *Let us pray:*

God our Father,
  we pray that we may grow
    in such a way
  as to be welcoming to other people,
  and generous in every way
  to those people we don't agree with.
Lead us to appreciate others
  in the same way
  that we would like to be appreciated.
Never let us look down on others,
  or consider anyone
  to be less than ourselves.
Show us how to be open-minded
  and able to learn from each other
  so that, together,
  we may grow as the people
  you invite us to be.
Amen.

3   Voltaire's words were:
    "I do not agree with what you say,
    but I would be prepared to die
    to defend your right to say it."

✍ *Voltaire expressed these words to Jean-Jacques Rousseau, another philosopher. Because of his views, Rousseau was being driven out from one place to another. Voltaire offered the hospitality of his own home to Rousseau. Voltaire spoke these words to him on arrival.*

1 John Henry Newman was born on this day in 1801. He became an Anglican priest and was a great religious thinker of his day. He lectured at Oxford University and influenced many. He was one of a group that became known as "the Oxford Movement". Although they had valued the Anglican Church, many left and became Roman Catholics.

2 Whilst still unsure of what he should do, Newman made a tour of the Mediterranean by ship in 1833. One of his poems is called "Lead Kindly Light", and it reflects on the time his fog-bound ship could see the distant lights of the French port of Marseilles.

3 As we are about to read Newman's poem, we can think of him struggling in darkness, unsure as to what he should do. Should he leave the Anglican Church and become a Roman Catholic? To do so would result in the loss of many of his friends. Newman asks Jesus, the Light of the world, to lead him on, just one step at a time. He is convinced that God has led him so far, and trusts that he will lead him in the future, even through further difficulties. Once life has ended, John will once again greet all who had been his friends ("those angel faces") whom he continued to love.

4 *Lead, kindly light, amid th'encircling gloom:*
lead thou me on.
The night is dark, and I am far from home,
lead thou me on.
Keep thou my feet; I do not ask to see
the distant scene; one step enough for me.

5 *I was not ever thus, nor prayed that thou*
shouldst lead me on.
I loved to choose and see my path; but now
lead thou me on.
I loved the garish day, and, 'spite of fears,
pride ruled my will; remember not past years.

6 *So long thy power hath blest me, sure it still*
will lead me on
o'er moor and fen, o'er crag and torrent,
* till the night is gone,*
and with the morn those angel faces smile
which I have loved long since and lost awhile.

7 Newman left the Anglican Church and became ordained as a Catholic priest. He was created a Cardinal in 1879, and died 11 years later.

✍ *"garish" in number 5 = showy*

✍ *" 'spite of" - in spite of.*

🎼 Be still and know I am with you; I watch the sunrise; Lead kindly light; The light of Christ; Walk in the light

1 We can think back to the days when we might have read the story of 'Peter Pan', or have seen a film (or even a pantomime!). In one scene the children have seen Peter fly, and they try to lift themselves into the air, but they can't manage to do what he does. They ask Peter, *"How do you do fly?"* Peter tells them, **"Think lovely thoughts."** They do, and then they achieve what they thought was impossible - they fly!

2 The story leaves us with the idea that we can do many things if only we *"think lovely thoughts"*, if only we "think positively" about things, "filling our minds" with good things.

3 In the Bible we find this passage from Saint Paul about filling our minds with good things.

"I want you to be happy,
always happy in the Lord.
I repeat, what I want is your happiness.
Let your tolerance be evident to everyone:
the Lord is very near.
There is no need to worry:
but if there is anything you need,
pray for it,
asking God for it
with prayer and thanksgiving,
and that peace of God,
which is so much greater
than we can understand,
will guard your hearts and your thoughts
in Christ Jesus.
Finally, fill your minds
with everything that is true,
everything that is noble,
everything that is good and pure,
everything that we love and honour,
and everything
that can be thought virtuous
or worthy of praise...
Then the God of peace will be with you."

4 *Let's pause for a moment in silent prayer, asking that our minds be filled with all that is good...*

🎵 *There is truth in the message of the song in "The Sound of Music" - I think of my favourite things, and then I don't feel so sad.*

🎵 *The author of Peter Pan was Sir James Barrie, and he wrote it in 1904.*

🎵 *The scripture is Philippians $4^{4\text{-}9}$: Jerusalem Bible*

♪ Give me joy in my heart

1 On this day in 1976 the English painter, L.S.Lowry, died. He painted scenes of mills and houses in the industrial towns of Manchester and Salford, painting in a simple, almost child-like way. He portrayed enormous factories and smoking chimneys that surrounded people whom he showed as small, stick-like figures. Lowry said of himself: *"I'm a simple man, and I use simple materials."* A song was written about Lowry and his paintings, called *"Matchstalk Men and Matchstalk Cats and Dogs".*

2 Thinking of the "little people" whom Lowry painted, we are reminded that if others saw anyone in the gospels as "small" or "insignificant", Jesus made them "walk tall".

3 Zacchaeus lived in Jericho. He was a small man who wanted others to look up to him, and he hoped to gain importance as a tax-collector. As Jesus walked along the road, crowds stood around him, and the small Zacchaeus could not see. He ran ahead and climbed a sycamore tree to make himself look bigger. As Jesus moved along, he not only looked at Zacchaeus, but called him by his name. Jesus arranged to eat in his house that night, showing the crowd that, whilst **they** had an attitude of rejecting Zacchaeus, he did not.

4 Let us pray:

Lord Jesus,
 you called Zacchaeus by his name
 and enabled him to grow.
I ask you to enter my life
 in a new way this day
 that I may grow
 in stature and wisdom and grace
 as the person you call me to be.

Inspire me to follow you more closely
 and help me to live in such a way
 that I encourage others
 and bring life to them.
No one is small in your eyes;
 let no one be small in mine.
Amen.

📖 *Lk 19$^{1-10}$ - Zacchaeus; Lk 15$^{4-10}$ - "little" animals/coins*

📖 *He is always referred to as "L.S.Lowry"; his Christian names were "Laurence Stephen".*

📖 *See also 18 July for similar ideas.*

1 Moslems are followers of the religion of "Islam" - a word that means *'surrender'* or *'submission to God.'*

2 Across the world, people of the religion of Islam set out to pray five times during the day. Before the start of prayer they prepare themselves and get into the right frame of mind. Preparation for prayer includes washing head and hands and feet - it is a sign of wanting to approach God in the right way, with the intention of being "clean" within. The prayer mat is spread towards Mecca in the east because that town has a special place of worship built by Abraham (whom we read of in the Old Testament). Moslems consider Abraham as their *"father in faith"* in the same way as do Jews and Christians.

3 Barefoot, the Moslem stands on the mat and begins to pray from their holy book, the Koran. Prayer starts with words in the Arabic language that are translated as: *"In the name of God, the Merciful, the Compassionate."* In humility before God, they then kneel and touch the ground with their foreheads, and say, *"God is great."* Personal prayers are added.

4 One of the five duties of Moslems is to pray five times each day - at dawn, midday, afternoon, evening and night. One thing that Moslems and Jews and Christians have in common, is that many pray several times throughout the day - even if it is just for a moment each time. People find that this helps them realise that they live in God's presence, and so their attitude is more likely to be positive and joyful and loving.

5 Let's spend a moment in silence - in common with many Moslems and Jews and Christians across the world - and simply call to mind that we are in God's presence - in the presence of God who cares for and loves each individual...

(pause...)

6 *We'll use as our prayer some words written by the father-in-law of Mohammad:*

I thank you, Lord,
for knowing me
better than I know myself.
I thank you for letting me know myself
better than others know me.
Make me, I ask you then,
better than they suppose I am,
and forgive me
for what they do not know.

🔊 *Praying at the prescribed times each day is called 'salat'.*

🔊 *Mohammed was the founder of Islam.*

🔊 *For paragraph 3, see 19 April.*

🔊 *The prayer was written by Abu Bakr, the father-in-law of Mohammad.*

🔊 *If anyone thinks that extremists in the Moslem world are "typical of all Moslems", ask if those who are violent and yet call themselves Christians in Northern Ireland, in the former Yugoslavia, in the Lebanon, and in Rwanda, are "typical of all Christians"!*

🔊 *Abraham - see Genesis 12-25*

🎵 Be still and know I am with you; In you, my God; I watch the sunrise; Oh the love of my Lord

1 In the same way that Moslems pray several times a day, many Christians feel the need to call to mind several times a day that they really are in the Presence of God. They remind themselves, for instance, that some of Jesus' last words after his Resurrection were:

"I will be with you until the end of time."

2 Some people find it helpful to learn a couple of lines of a prayer, and simply repeat them slowly a few times a day. That is a way of reminding themselves that they are in the Presence of God who calls them by name and loves them.

3 *Let us pray, using some words from one of the psalms in the Bible:*

**I thank you, Lord,
for the wonder of myself,
and for the wonders of all your creation.**
(Psalm 139)

4 This prayer is so short that it can be memorised and simply repeated at odd moments during the day, and no-one else would ever know that you were praying. Some people find it's helpful to do this with a very short prayer, simply repeating it slowly a few times throughout the day. It is a way that many people use to grow in the awareness that God is with them. They realise that, if they really live in God's presence, they can only be positive and joyful and loving.

> **I thank you, Lord,
> for the wonder of myself,
> and for the wonders of all your creation.**
> *(Psalm 139)*

📖 *Some examples of short phrases to memorise and use as occasional prayers:*

**I thank you
for your faithfulness and love.
You stretch out your hand
and save me.**
(Psalm 137/138)

**Jesus, remember me
when you come into your kingdom.**
(Luke 23⁴²)

Lord, you know that I love you.
(John 17)

**The things, good Lord, that we pray for,
give us your grace to work for.**
(St Thomas More)

**Let us remember
that we are in the presence of God.
And let us adore him.**

In which year was the Great Fire of London?
(1666)

Where did it start?
(In a baker's shop in Pudding Lane).

Why did the Fire spread so quickly?
(Most buildings were wooden, and were very close to each other).

How did the Fire stop eventually?
(In some areas the fire burned itself out when all the buildings had been destroyed. In other places, King Charles II's brother - who would become King James II - ordered that houses in the path of the fire should be blown up, so that there would be a gap, a "firebreak").

Some people thought that the Fire must be a great punishment for what they must have done wrong. They had all the more reason to think this because another great disaster had hit them, starting two years earlier in 1664. What was that disaster?
(The Great Plague, killing 75,000 in London alone).

The Great Fire of London destroyed the oldest part of the city. After the Fire, King Charles II ordered that special buildings be re-built, one of which was St Paul's Cathedral, which bears a large dome. Who was the famous architect of St Paul's Cathedral?
(Sir Christopher Wren).

1   It was on this day in 1723 that Sir Christopher Wren died. In St Paul's, people can read an inscription about Christopher Wren near his tomb. The words were written by his son:

*"If you seek his monument,
look around you."*

2   Those words about Sir Christopher Wren - *"If you seek his monument, look around you"* - remind us to be aware of how we are building our lives.

3   *Let us pray:*

Lord, be the foundation
on which I build my life.
May my door be wide enough
that I may be welcoming,
inviting others to grow.
May my door be narrow enough
to keep out what is not good.
May I build no walls
that keep anyone out,
but build your Kingdom
together with all whom you give me
as my brothers and sisters -
valuing all who are a part of my life.
May I live in such a way
that those "who trespass against" me
- who hurt me -
may know my forgiveness and generosity
- as I know yours.
Surround me with your love
and shield me from all harm.
Amen.

> *"If you seek his monument,
> look around you."*

✥•✥•✥•✥•✥•✥•✥•✥•✥•✥•✥•✥•✥•✥•✥

✍ *Does my own room/space say something about me?*

✍ *If I was to die tomorrow, what few words might I like others to use that would reflect my life?*

✍ *Some of the inhabitants of St Helena - an island in the South Atlantic Ocean - are descended from Londoners made homeless during the 1666 Great Fire of London, who were then shipped to the island.*

 For I'm building a people of power

1 In 1945 the United Nations was established, and building began in New York
for their headquarters, on land set aside
by the United States. On this day in 1952
the first session was held in the new
United Nations building in New York. On
the front of that building appear words
from the Bible found in the prophet
Isaiah:

2 *"They will hammer their swords*
so that they become ploughs.
Their spears will be forged
into pruning-hooks.
Nations will never go to war again;
there will be no more training for war."

3 Instruments of war will be changed into
instruments of agriculture - an attitude
of war will be transformed into an attitude of peace.

4 Let's pray for peace in parts of our world
where there is war and violence and
bloodshed. We pray in the words of what
is called *"The Universal Prayer for Peace"*
- a prayer that is used in many countries
and in many different languages:

5 **O God,**
lead us from death to life,
from falsehood to truth.
Lead us from despair to hope,
from fear to trust.
Lead us from hate to love,
from war to peace.
Let peace fill our hearts,
our world, our universe. Amen.
('The Universal Prayer of Peace')

The text in Isaiah 2^{2-5} is much the same as that in Micah 4^{1-4}.

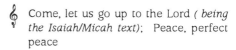

Come, let us go up to the Lord (*being the Isaiah/Micah text)*; Peace, perfect peace

1 The words *"Do not be afraid"* appear 366 times throughout the whole of the Bible - as though it is a daily message for each day of a leap year. *"Do not be afraid"* is a very basic message of the Bible.

2 The angel tells Mary not to be afraid when she is asked to be the mother of Jesus. Joseph is told not to be afraid, but to take Mary as his wife, and the shepherds in the fields were told not to be afraid.

3 Jesus calls Simon Peter to follow him, telling him not to be afraid. When Jesus walks on the water towards his disciples in their boat, he sees what they are like and says: *"Have courage, don't be afraid; it's me!"*

4 Jesus says: *"No one is forgotten in God's sight. There's no need to be afraid, because you are precious. Don't worry about the future."* When Jesus rises from the dead, he says to his friends: *"Don't be afraid...I leave you my peace."*

5 Let's pause for a moment in silence, remembering that God calls each of us by name and tells each of us not to be afraid. Let's pause for a moment and each simply repeat those words in silence a few times - *"Do not be afraid"* - starting with our own name.

(pause...)

✍ *"Angel" means "God's messenger"*

✍ *Lk 1^{30} - Mary;*
Mt 1^{20} - Joseph;
Lk 5^{10} - Simon Peter;

✍ *Lk 14^{27} - water;*
Lk 12$^{7-32}$ - precious;

✍ *Mt 28^{10}/Jn 14^{27} - resurrection)*

♩ Do not be afraid; Be not afraid

1 Every four years we have a leap year, adding a day - 29th February.

2 Let's think of those who look back and wish they had an extra day or **more time**:
- those who have too little time
  for what they are expected to do;
- those who have lost a sense of balance
  and proportion in their lives;
- those who feel
  that they have made a mess
  of everything
  and would like to be able to start again.

3 We pray, too,
  for those who might wish for **less time**:
- those who are worried
  about what might happen;
- those who are in despair;
- those who suffer hours
  of pain and illness;
- those who are in prison
  or are being tortured;
- those who wish to die

4 **On all these people, Lord,
  we ask your blessing.**

✍ Could use Michel Quoist's prayer, "Lord, I have time" from his book, "Prayers of Life".

✍ Century years divisible by 400 are leap years - e.g. 2000. Other century years are not leap years - e.g. 1900

✍ See also 23 March

1 Today is the feast of Saint David, the Patron of Wales. He lived in the south-west corner of Wales, and founded several monasteries. He died about the year 588 in his own monastery of Menevia, where he was also bishop. After his death, the village was re-named "St Davids". Although only a village, St Davids has a huge cathedral - technically making it a city.

2 We pray today for all Welsh people. Some will be wearing a daffodil, being one of the national emblems of the country.

3 As the month of March begins, we can pause for a moment in silence to think of some of the signs that remind us that winter is past, and spring is upon us - signs such as daffodils and other bulbs that have flowered...

(pause)

4 *Let us pray:*

Lord of life,
 we give you thanks
 for the beauty of creation,
 and we rejoice
 when we see signs of new life.
May we be Spring to others
 and never Winter.
Amen.

✍ *Some signs of spring: bulbs and flowers; birdsong; lengthening days; knowing that the warmth and sunlight of summer are approaching; weather and temperature; people's optimism and cheerfulness.*

✍ *In Welsh, "Saint David" is "Dewi Sant".*

♦ Guide me, O thou great Redeemer; I watch the sunrise; Laudato sii; Morning has broken; Thank you for fathers

1 The story of Jonah and the whale is found in the Old Testament. It is probably best read as a parable - a story with a message.

2 God spoke to Jonah: *"Get up and go to Nineveh, that great city."* *"No way,"* thought Jonah. *"It's not for me to go to the capital city of the Assyrians, our hated enemies."* Jonah boarded a ship that would go in the opposite direction. Out to sea, a severe storm blew up. Each sailor prayed to his god - they were about to drown. Jonah came forward: *"It's my fault you're in this trouble; the storm will stop if you throw me overboard."* Reluctantly they did, and a great fish swallowed him whole. Jonah had three days to think about himself, and then the fish spat him out. Where? On the shore near Nineveh!

3 God spoke to him a second time: *"Jonah, go to Nineveh."* This time he obeyed. He walked into that great city and said: *"God's message is that this city will be destroyed in 40 days' time because you live in a wicked way."*

4 What a surprise for Jonah that the people really listened to him. Word even reached the king. They all took the message seriously and turned away from all the wrong they had been doing, and God spared the city.

5 What was Jonah's reaction? He was angry with God and said: *"That's why I ran away. I knew you'd be kind and merciful - that's the way you are."* The cold-hearted Jonah sulked; he'd wanted to see the foreigners and their city destroyed. Jonah was only concerned about himself.

6 He sat outside the city in the burning heat of the sun. He was glad that God had made a plant grow to shade his head, but the next day a worm attacked the plant and it died - and so Jonah no longer had any shade from the fierce heat. *"I could die with anger,"* said Jonah. But God said: *"You are angry - not at the loss of a single person - but at the loss of a plant that you only cared for because it was doing something for you. Learn the lesson that I care for and treasure all people - without exception. Learn the lesson that, unlike you, I'm not prejudiced against people who are different from you. Learn the lesson that I'm more kind and merciful than you will ever be. Learn from your experience."*

7 *Let's pause for a moment in silence...*

(pause...)

📖 *The short Book of Jonah is in the Old Testament.*

📖 *'Assyria' covered parts of present-day Iran, Iraq and Syria. The city of Nineveh would have been about 300 miles north of present-day Baghdad.*

🎼 Be still and know I am with you; Father, in my life I see; For to those who love God; I am with you forever; If God is for us

1 Late one afternoon the composer Beethoven visited a shoemaker. Standing in the shop, waiting to have his shoes mended, Beethoven heard some music being played on a piano in the back room of the shop. Beethoven smiled, knowing that the music was one of his own compositions. *"It's my daughter who's playing"*, said the shoemaker, *"but she can't play very well because she is blind and has to play from memory."*

2 *"May I play the piano for your daughter? I am a musician myself,"* asked Beethoven. *"Certainly"*, said the shoemaker, not knowing who his customer was. Beethoven slowly rehearsed the music with the girl, and they began to practice other pieces he had written (although the girl was not aware that her teacher was, in fact, the composer). The time went quickly, and Beethoven didn't realise that hours had passed. Then he noticed the way that the moonlight had begun to stream its gentle light through the window of the room.

3 Beethoven returned home. He couldn't get to sleep, but thought of how the girl was disabled by blindness, struggling to do her best, whilst others took sight and talents for granted. He thought of the great joy that music brought her, and he remembered the room in which they had played the music, and the way in which the moonlight streamed through the open window. He knew that whilst <u>he</u> could see the moonlight, she could not. Beethoven got out of bed and started to play the piano, expressing his feelings through music.

4 What he produced is thought by many to be one of the most touching pieces of music. In memory of the girl, he called this new piece *"The Moonlight Sonata"*.

On this day in 1802, the music of Beethoven's *"Moonlight Sonata"* was published.

5 *Let us pray:*

**Lord, you have watched me grow
in my mother's womb,
and I know that you love
all that you have made.
Help me to transform
my difficulties and disabilities
into opportunities for growth.
Shine the light of your Spirit on me
that I may grow
as the person you are calling me to be.
Inspire me
to develop the talents
you have given me
for the benefit and the service
of those people
you have placed in my life.
May each of us
become a blessing for others.
Amen.**

✍ *Ludwig Van Beethoven was born in Bonn, Germany, 16/12/1770; he died in Vienna, Austria, 26/3/1827. See also 28 April and 7 May.*

✍ *Beethoven struggled with increasing deafness, often not being able to hear the music he was composing. "I shall hear in heaven," he said.*

✍ *Today is the anniversary in 1996 of the murder of 16 primary school children and their teacher, Gwen Mayor, in Dunblane, near Stirling, Scotland.*

♪ Be still and know I am with you; I watch the sunrise; I will never forget you; Lay your hands

4 MARCH

1 Abraham Lincoln was elected 16th President of the United States. On this day in 1861 he was sworn in as President, just as the American Civil War was about to begin. He is one of the most respected of American presidents, but he could have given up at the time of any one of his many failures and negative experiences:

2 In 1832 he was defeated in state elections. In 1833 he failed as a shopkeeper and was in debt.
1836 saw him have a nervous breakdown. In 1849 he was disillusioned at not being offered a government post, and he left politics for a time.
In 1855 and also in 1858 he was defeated in his wish to be elected for the U.S. Senate.

3 He experienced personal tragedy as three of his four children died young. On finally becoming president, he was let down by some of those he had appointed to positions of trust.

4 *Let us pray:*

Father,
into your hands I place my successes.
Into your hands
  I also place my failures,
  and I pray that, through your Spirit,
  I may face the challenges of life
  with courage and determination.
Help me to think anew
  and see things more broadly
  than in terms of "success"
  and "failure".
Lead me always to trust
  and place myself confidently
  in your hands.
Amen.

Abraham Lincoln was born 12/2/1809, and died 15/4/1865, the day after being shot.

Mother Teresa said of 'success':
"I don't remember
that the Lord ever spoke of success.
He spoke only of faithfulness in loving.
The Lord has called me to faithfulness in love.
This is the only success that really counts".

Psalm 30/31 and Luke 23[46]
- "Into your hands I commend my spirit".

Abba, Father, you are the potter; Father, in my life I see; Father I place into your hands

1 William Penn was born in England in 1644. He was a member of the 'Quakers', 'The Society of Friends'. A focus of their form of Christianity is the equality of everyone. They live simply, and they refuse to fight.

2 At a time when Britain still governed North America, William Penn was granted land by King Charles II *(the second)*, in return for a large sum of money owed him by the king. It was a great forested area called "Sylvania" after the Latin name for a wood. The king insisted that Penn add his own name, and the colony (now one of the United States of America) became known as "Pennsylvania".

3 Penn and his followers were empowered by the king to fight and make war against those considered to be "Indian savages", but to fight would have been against their religion. Penn refused to build any forts or fight against the Native Americans. Nor would he have any soldiers in the colony. People who weren't Quakers soon said that they would be slaughtered by the Native American tribes. Instead the Quakers began to build their town, calling it "Philadelphia", from Greek words meaning "the city of brotherly love". Both communities of people made friends with each other. They agreed that, if any problems arose, they should sort them out at a meeting of equal numbers of Native Americans and British settlers. Both groups of people lived in equality, sharing the same rights. When William Penn died, he was mourned by them all.

4 Pennsylvania remained free from attack as long as the settlers did not arm themselves. Once the Quakers were outvoted in the State, and forts were built and men trained as soldiers - only then were they attacked.

5 *Let's pray*
in the words of St Francis of Assisi:

Lord, make me an instrument
of your peace:
where there is hatred,
let me sow love;
where there is injury, pardon;
where there is doubt, faith;
where there is despair, hope;
where there is darkness, light;
and where there is sadness, joy.
O Divine Master,
grant that I may not so much seek
to be consoled, as to console;
to be understood, as to understand;
to be loved, as to love.
For it is in giving that we receive,
it is in pardoning
that we are pardoned,
and it is in dying
that we are born to eternal life.
Amen.

🔊 *See 13 March for an alternative prayer.*

🔊 *Those who used to be called 'Indians' are often now known as 'Native Americans'. The film, "Dances with Wolves", starring Kevin Costner, tells of the Native Americans being exploited and then killed by the white soldiers.*

🔊 *William Penn was born in London, 14/10/1644; he died in Buckinghamshire, England, 30/7/1718.*

🔊 *See the notes on 24 January regarding Quakers.*

🔊 *John 14[27] - my peace I give you; a peace the world cannot give.*

♪ Come, let us go up to the Lord; Lord, make me a means; Make me a channel

6 MARCH

1 The ancient Greeks discovered that the bark of the willow tree provided medicine. Native Americans made the same discovery. It is the salicylic acid in the bark of the willow tree that counters fever and pain.

2 A German chemist, Felix Hoffman, produced a slight variation of this acid that is not as bitter as the original, nor as irritating to the stomach. On this day in 1899 he patented his compound - no one could copy it without his permission - and he called it ASPIRIN.

3 We know that aspirin is one of the medicines that may be taken for pain. Those who suffer from arthritis and rheumatism sometimes take it, and it is helpful to those with long-term heart problems. Research has shown that it also helps reduce the risk of some forms of cancer.

4 Let us pray that people be inspired to appreciate all that is good and beneficial around them. Let us pray that good decisions be reached concerning the environment - decisions that look to our heritage as well as to our needs.

Lord, in your mercy - **hear our prayer.**

5 Let us pray for those who are concerned about their health and their future. We pray for people in physical pain, for those who make little progress, and for those who will never get better.

Lord, in your mercy - **hear our prayer.**

6 Let us pray for all who are sad, and for all who have had bitter experiences in their lives. Let us pray that we may be protected from all that may harm us.

Lord, in your mercy - **hear our prayer.**

📖 *The derivative is acetylsalicylic acid = aspirin. As aspirin thins the blood, it is taken regularly by some people with heart problems, being a means of preventing clotting of the blood.*

📖 *The film, 'The Medicine Man', starring Sean Connery, concerns the destruction of rain forests at the expense not only of the local people but also of medicinal cures.*

 Lay your hands

1 The second Monday in March is "**Commonwealth Day**". The "**Commonwealth of Nations**" is an association of some 53 independent nations, including over a quarter of the world's population. In years past, all the countries have been associated with Britain - except for Mozambique (formerly a Portuguese colony) which joined in 1995, having seen how the Commonwealth helps to give a voice to some small or poor countries.

2 We can think today of how unique is each and every individual in the world. We'll pray the shortest psalm in the Bible. It invites people - not of any **single** country, but the people of **all** nations - to give praise to God:

3 *Let us pray:*

**Praise the Lord, all you nations.
Speak to him, all people of the earth,
because his love is great
and he is always faithful.**

(Psalm 117)

✍ *Alternative prayer: as of 21 March.*

✍ *The 53 independent countries of the Commonwealth are:*

Antigua and Barbuda (joined in 1981), in the West Indies, the Caribbean.
Australia (1931).
The Bahamas (1973), West Indies, the Caribbean.
Bangladesh (1972), Asia.
Barbados (1966), West Indies, the Caribbean.
Belize (1981), north eastern Central America.
Botswana (1966), southern Africa.
Brunei (1984), part of the island of Borneo, eastern Asia.
Cameroon (1995), west central Africa (most of the country is a former French colony).
Canada (1931), northern America.
Cyprus (1961), in the Mediterranean.
Dominica (1978), West Indies, the Caribbean.
The Gambia (1965), north western Africa.
Ghana (1957), western Africa.
Grenada (1974), West Indies, the Caribbean
Guyana (1966), northern coast of South America.
India (1947), Asia.
Jamaica (1962), West Indies, the Caribbean.
Kenya (1963), eastern Africa.
Kiribati (1979), islands 2,100 miles north east of Australia.
Lesotho (1966), southern Africa.
Malawi (1964), south eastern Africa.
Malaysia (1957), Asia.
Maldives (1982), islands off the south west coast of India.
Malta (1964), in the Mediterranean.
Mauritius (1968), island near Madagascar, off eastern Africa.
Mozambique (1995), south east Africa; it was formerly a Portuguese colony with no British connections.
Namibia (1990), south western Africa.
Nauru (1968), island 2,500 miles north east of Australia.
New Zealand (1931), 1,200 miles south east of Australia.
Nigeria (1960), Africa; membership suspended in 1995.
Pakistan (1947, left 1972, rejoined 1989), Asia.

Papua New Guinea (1975), off northern Australia.
St Christopher (Kitts) and Nevis (1983), West Indies, the Caribbean.
St Lucia (1979), West Indies, the Caribbean.
St Vincent and the Grenadines (1979), West Indies, the Caribbean.
The Seychelles (1979), islands 900 miles off western Africa.
Sierra Leone (1961), on western coast of Africa.
Singapore (1965), Asia.
The Solomon Islands (1978), 1000 miles north east of Australia.
South Africa (1931, left 1961, rejoined 1994).
Sri Lanka (1948), island off south east coast of India.
Swaziland (1968), east of South Africa.
Tanzania (1961), on eastern coast of Africa.
Tonga (1970), island 2,000 miles north east of Australia.
Trinidad and Tobago (1962), a Caribbean island just off the coast of Venezuela.
Tuvalu (1978), islands 2,000 miles off coast of north east Australia.
Uganda (1962), central Africa.
United Kingdom
Vanuatu (1980), islands 1,000 miles off the north eastern coast of Australia. Formerly called the 'New Hebrides' which was a joint British/French territory.
Western Samoa (1970), islands 3,000 miles off the north eastern coast of Australia.
Zambia (1964), southern Africa.
Zimbabwe (1980), southern Africa.

✍ *"The Commonwealth of Nations" was formerly called "The British Commonwealth". Fiji withdrew from the Commonwealth in 1987, and Nigeria was suspended in 1995. The British monarch is the Head of the Commonwealth.*

✍ *Only independent nations can be members of the Commonwealth, but self-governing or dependent territories of member countries are within the Commonwealth. In addition to the 53 independent nations, therefore, are such as the 13 dependencies of Britain e.g. Bermuda, Montserrat (where the volcano erupted in 1997), Cayman Islands, Falkland Islands,*

Gibraltar, Pitcairn Islands. Members of the Commonwealth have "High Commissions" rather than "Embassies" in each others' countries. Every two years there is a formal meeting of the Heads of Government of the countries of the Commonwealth.

✍ *The Isle of Man and the Channel Islands are dependencies of the British crown rather than of Britain itself, and are not actually part of the United Kingdom. They have their own government and do not have representation in the Westminster Parliament. They are not members of the Commonwealth of Nations, nor of the European Community.*

✍ *The facts given here are as of August 1997. For further details, the Commonwealth Secretariat can be contacted at Marlborough House, Pall Mall, London SW1Y 5HX.*

♪ All the nations of the earth; Come let us go up to the Lord; Follow me; O Lord, all the world

1 This is the birthday of the author, Kenneth Grahame, who wrote the book *"The Wind in the Willows"* In that book, two of the characters, Rat and Mole, paddle the boat upriver very early one morning. As the sun rises, they sense that they are in the Presence of some Divine Being, and they feel called to worship:

2 *'Slowly, but with no doubt or hesitation whatever, and in something of a solemn expectancy, the two animals passed through the broken, tumultuous water, and moored their boat at the flowery margin of the island. In silence they landed, and pushed through the blossom and scented herbage and undergrowth that led up to the level ground, till they stood on a little lawn of a marvellous green, set round with Nature's own orchard-trees: crab-apple, wild cherry, and sloe.*

3 "This is the place of my song-dream, the place the music played to me," *whispered Rat, as if in a trance.* "Here, in this holy place, here if anywhere, surely we shall find Him!"

4 *Then suddenly Mole felt a great Awe fall upon him, an awe that turned his muscles to water, bowed his head, and rooted his feet to the ground. It was no panic terror - indeed, he felt wonderfully at peace, and happy - but it was an awe that smote and held him and, without seeing, he knew it could only mean that some PRESENCE was very, very near. With difficulty he turned to look for his friend, and saw him at his side, cowed, stricken, and trembling violently. And still there was utter silence in the populous bird-haunted branches around them; and still the light grew and grew.*

5 "Rat!" *he found breath to whisper, shaking.* "Are you afraid?" "Afraid?" *murmured the Rat, his eyes shining with unutterable love.* "Afraid! Of Him? O, never, never! And yet - and yet - O Mole, I am afraid!" *Then the two animals, crouching to the earth, bowed their heads, and did worship.'*

6 Let's remind ourselves in silence that God is with us and we are in his presence...

(pause...)

📖 *In a poll in January 1997 to list the 100 Greatest Books of the 20th Century, 'The Wind in the Willows' came 16th.*

📖 *Kenneth Grahame was born in Edinburgh in 1859, and died in 1932.*

🎼 Be not afraid; Christ be beside me; Do not be afraid; I am with you forever; In you my God; Oh the love of my Lord; This day God gives me

9 MARCH

1   *"The sun is so large*
   that, if it were hollow, it could contain
   more than a million worlds
   of the size of our earth.
   There are stars in space so large
   that they could easily hold
   500 million suns of the size of ours."

2   Let's pause and think for a moment how
   small we are in the Universe, yet we can
   read in the Bible that God has written
   the name of each of us on the palm of
   his hand...

   (pause...)

3   *Let us pray:*

   Lord God,
   Creator of light,
   at the rising of your sun each morning
   let the greatest of all lights - your love
   - rise, like the sun, within my heart.

📖 *Isaiah 49 - name written on the palm of his hand.*

📖 *Psalm 8 - see version printed for 12 April.*

📖 *The sun uses up 4 million tons of hydrogen every second, but the sun is expected to last another 10,000 million years. The mass of the sun is 99% of the total mass of our solar system.*

📖 *The quote is from Morris Mandell.*

🎼 I will never forget you; I watch the sunrise; O Lord my God, the Father of creation; O Lord my God, when I in awesome wonder

1 Alexander Graham Bell is probably best remembered for having been the person who invented the telephone.

2 He was born in Scotland but moved to Canada and then the United States. In Boston he set up a training school for those who would teach the deaf. Trying to invent a machine that would help deaf people to hear, he learned how to use electricity as a means of transmitting speech.

3 It was on this day - 10th March - in the year 1876, that wires were laid between two rooms, and the first words were spoken on a telephone. They were addressed by Alexander Graham Bell to his assistant: *"Mr Watson, will you please come up here? I want you."*

4 Sometimes we take many things for granted - like the telephone. There are times, too, when we take people for granted.

5 Let us pray
that each of us develops
the skills and talents
we have been given,
and that we remain open and sensitive
to all that is around us.

Lord, hear us - *Lord, graciously hear us.*

6 Let us pray that we may live in such a way
that we use things and love people,
instead of using people
and loving things.

Lord, hear us - *Lord, graciously hear us.*

7 We pray that we may value and treasure
all who come into our lives
- not just for what they can do,
but for who they are.
Let us pray that we live in such a way
as to express appreciation

by the way we look at people
and in what we say.

Lord, hear us - *Lord, graciously hear us.*

Alexander Graham Bell was born in Edinburgh on 3/3/1847, and died in Canada, 2/8/1922. He was a friend of Helen Keller - see 1/3 June.

I give my hands; Take my hands

11 MARCH

(See also 9 January)

1 It was about 1890 when the Churchill family visited friends who had a large house and a swimming pool. The children went for a swim, and one of them - Winston Churchill - began to drown in the pool. The others screamed for help. Into the pool jumped the son of the gardener of the house, and he rescued the lad. Winston Churchill's parents were so grateful to the gardener's lad that they asked his parents what they might do for him in return. "He wants to be a doctor," they said.

2 The Churchills agreed to pay his way through college so that he could train as a doctor. He would became world-famous as Sir Alexander Fleming, the person who discovered penicillin.

3 In 1943, at the height of the Second World War, Winston Churchill - who, by then, was the British Prime Minister - met with President Roosevelt of the United States and Soviet leader Joseph Stalin. After the meeting, Winston Churchill was struck down with pneumonia, which was likely to kill him. King George VI *(the sixth)* insisted that the best doctor in the country look after him, and so Dr Alexander Fleming - the same person who had rescued Churchill from drowning as a boy - now treated him for his life-threatening pneumonia.

4 Churchill said to Fleming: *"Rarely has one man owed his life twice to the same rescuer."*

5 Today is the anniversary of the death of Alexander Fleming - 11th March 1955.

6 *Let's reflect and pray:*

I shall pass through this world but once.
Therefore, any good that I can do,
   any kind act that I can perform
   for any fellow-creature,
   let me do it now.
Let me not delay or omit it,
   for I shall not pass this way again.

(attributed to Stephen Grellet)

✍ *The meeting was held in the capital of Iran. The 'Tehran Conference' was to review how the War was progressing, and to discuss the shape of Europe after the War.*

✍ *Alexander Fleming: 1881-1955*
Winston Churchill: 1874-1965.

 Lay your hands

1 In Amsterdam, the capital of German-occupied Holland in the Second World War, Anne Frank and her family and four other Jews hid from the Nazis in concealed rooms in what had been her father's offices. For more than two years they were secure there, unknown to those who worked in the building, except for a friend who arranged to get food to them. They were betrayed in 1944, and all eight were sent to the death camps. Only Anne's father - Otto Frank - survived and returned.

2 Anne died of typhus in the concentration camp of Bergen-Belsen on this day, 12th March, 1945, aged 15. Only weeks later the camp was liberated.

3 Anne Frank's story is now known to millions across the world because of the diary that she kept about her innermost thoughts during those years in hiding. Her father discovered the diary on his return to their hiding-place, once the war ended. 'The Diary of Anne Frank' has sold 25 million copies, and has been printed in over 50 languages.

4 This is an excerpt from Anne's diary, dated Saturday 15th July 1944:

5 *"It's really a wonder that I haven't dropped all my ideals because they seem so absurd and impossible to carry out. Yet I keep them, because in spite of everything I still believe that people are really good at heart. I simply can't build up my hopes on a foundation consisting of confusion, misery, and death. I see the world gradually being turned into a wilderness. I hear the ever-approaching thunder, which will destroy us, too. I can feel the suffering of millions and yet, if I look up into the heavens, I think that it will all come right, that this cruelty, too, will end, and that peace and tranquility will return again. In the meantime, I must uphold my ideals, for perhaps the time will come when I shall be able to carry them out."*

6 Let us pause for a moment in silent prayer, thinking of all who suffer prejudice and persecution because of their race, colour, religion or political views...

(pause...)

God our Father,
 you call each of us by name
 and you know
  the innermost thoughts
 that we keep to ourselves.
Stay with us, day by day,
 in good times and in bad.
Empower us with your Spirit
 that we may grow in character
 and develop a true sense of values
  and ideals
 through following Jesus,
 your Son and our Brother.
Amen.

In a poll in January 1997 to list the 100 Greatest Books of the 20th Century, 'The Diary of Anne Frank' came 26th. The book has been made into a film.

Be not afraid; Do not be afraid; Father, I place into your hands; For to those who love God; He who would valiant be

13 MARCH

1 The people of Argentina and Chile were preparing for war because of a dispute over which country owned some land high in the Andes mountains that separated the two countries. On Easter Sunday many people gathered in the cathedral of Buenos Aires, the capital of Argentina. The bishop preached in his sermon about the need for peace. Many disagreed with him, but some supported him - including a bishop in the opposing country of Chile who went about his own country, also preaching peace.

2 Such was the effect of the two bishops on the people of their countries, that the two governments felt they should step back from war and talk with each other again. They agreed to invite King Edward VII *(the seventh)* of Britain to make a decision about who should own the land over which they were about to go to war.

3 The bishop from Argentina had said: *"I would like to see Christ standing between our two nations, guiding us and leading us."* Some people decided to take this literally and set about fund-raising to build a statue of Christ. On this day - 13th March - 1904, representatives of both countries gathered around the huge statue that had been built on one of the mountains of the Andes, between both nations. This is one of the prayers used: *"that these great mountains may crumble into dust before the peoples of Argentina and Chile break the peace which we have promised to keep, here at the feet of Christ."*

4 The huge statue of "Christ of the Andes" is a great symbol and reminder of the need to work together for peace.

5 *Let us pray:*

Lord,
   inspire us to act justly, love tenderly,
   and walk humbly with you, our God.
Breathe upon us your Spirit of peace
   that we may be
   bearers of reconciliation
   wherever you place us.
May there be peace in our hearts,
   in our homes, in our land,
   and between all people.
Amen.

🔖 *For an alternative prayer, see 5 March*

🔖 *The first part of the prayer "Act justly..." is from the Biblical book of Micah 6^8.*

🔖 *Micah 4^{1-7}/Isaiah 2^{2-5} - Let us go up to the mountain of the Lord; ploughshares into pruning hooks; nation shall not lift up sword against nation.*

🔖 *John 14^{27} - my peace I give you; a peace the world cannot give.*

🔖 *The statue of Christ of the Andes is not to be confused with the statue of Christ overlooking Rio de Janeiro, Brazil.*

🔖 *Edward VII was King of the United Kingdom from 1901-1910.*

🎵 Come, let us go up to the Lord; Make me a channel; Lord, make me a means; Though the mountains may fall.

(See also 18 April & 18 May)

1 Born on this day in 1879 was Albert Einstein, who became one of the most brilliant scientists. He found that his studies of science led him closer to God, and he wrote:

2 *"The most beautiful thing*
that we can experience
is the MYSTERIOUS.
It is the only source of true art and science.
And those to whom this emotion is a stranger
- those who can no longer
pause in WONDER
or stand wrapt in AWE -
they are already dead:
their eyes are shut."

3 *Let us pray:*

Father, preserve in us
a sense of wonder
at the marvels of life.
May all that we see around us
lead us to you. Amen.

📖 *Albert Einstein - who also said:* "God does not play dice with the world" *- was born in Germany in 1879, and died in 1955 in the USA.*

📖 *Einstein also wrote:*

"Everyone who is seriously involved
in the pursuit of science
becomes convinced
that a spirit is manifested
in the laws of the Universe -
a Spirit vastly superior to that of man,
and one in the face of which
we, with our modest powers,
must feel humble."

See the first paragraph of the Introduction
for references to 'wonder'.

🎼 Amazing grace; Christ be beside me; I watch the sunrise; Lord of all hopefulness; Morning has broken; Oh the love of my Lord; O Lord my God, when I in awesome wonder

15 MARCH

1 On 15th March 1877 the first Test Match in cricket was held: Australia and England played in Melbourne, Australia.

2 It was five years later, in 1882, that England unexpectedly lost the Test Match at home against Australia. One of the newspapers reported the great shock - England had lost in the sport that the country had invented. The following "obituary" notice appeared in 'The Sporting Times':

3 "In affectionate remembrance of English Cricket which died at the Oval on 29th August 1882. Deeply lamented by a large circle of sorrowing friends and acquaintances R.I.P.. The body will be cremated and the ashes taken to Australia."

4 Later that year, an English team in Australia was presented with an urn containing ashes. That trophy is now kept permanently at Lord's cricket ground in London. The phrase has remained: whoever wins the Test Match is said to have won "the Ashes".

5 I can think of times
    when others have let me down.
I remember when I have let others down.

6 I can think of times
    when people expected too much of me.
I remember
    when I haven't expected enough
        of myself.

7 I can think of times
    when I haven't felt appreciated.
I remember when I haven't praised others
    for the good use of their talents.

8 *And so we pray:*

May we learn
    to value and appreciate one another,
    bringing out the best
        in those around us.
May what is not good
    die within us,
    and may we bring life to all we meet.
Amen.

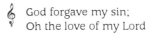 God forgave my sin;
Oh the love of my Lord

MARCH 16

1 In an article in the *'Observer'* newspaper in 1992, it was stated that Britain had enough wheat and barley lying unused in government-funded storage to feed the starving country of Somalia in Africa for more than a year.

2 Farmers are subsidised to grow food; some farmers are subsidised <u>not</u> to grow food - on what is called "set-aside" land. The European Union's "food mountains" (as they are sometimes called) include grain, milk powder, butter, wine, and meat. Money is paid to keep these products in storage. Because they are not used, the price of food is kept high.

3 The European Union has so much wheat in storage that a newspaper calculated that, if baked into bread, all that wheat could form a single slice of bread 1000 miles wide by 1000 miles long, covering all of Europe!

4 *Let us pray for the needy and hungry of our world:*

God our Father,
  we think of the beauty of the world
  which you proclaimed to be good,
  but we are also conscious
    of our misuse
  of what you have given to us.
Our governments
  spend money in our name
  maintaining "butter mountains"
  and "wine lakes",
  and we subsidise farmers
    to "set aside" land
  so that less food is produced
  - even though
    our brothers and sisters
  die each day from hunger.
On our paper money
  we print the images
    of famous people,
yet often do not treasure and uphold
the dignity of all who are made
in your image and likeness.

5 Open our hearts
  to be influenced for good,
  and inspire us
  to touch the hearts of others.
Enable us to change the things
  that contradict your love,
  and may all your people
  work and grow together
  as brothers and sisters.
Amen.

📖 *CAFOD, Romero Close, Stockwell Road, London SW9 TY*

📖 *Tear Fund, 100 Church Road, Teddington, Middlesex, TW11 8QE*

🎼 I give my hands; O Lord all the world

1 Today is the feast of St Patrick, Patron of Ireland. We pray this day for all Irish people.

2 Patrick was born about the year 400AD - either near what is now the English/Scottish border (in what was then the Province of Britannia in the Roman Empire), or near the River Severn by the present English/Welsh border. Wherever he was born, he was captured by raiders, made a slave and taken to Ireland when he was about 16 years old. There he was forced to work in the fields, looking after sheep and pigs. He managed to escape in a ship which took him to France. Some time later he became a priest and then a bishop.

3 He returned to his birthplace and had a vivid dream or a vision, calling him to return to Ireland and take the Gospel to the people there.

4 It was as a young man (and whilst he was a captive) that he had much time to think and reflect, and he grew in his relationship with God. Spending days and nights in the open countryside, looking after the animals, he became more and more aware that God was there with him. Patrick learned to live in the Presence of God.

6 Let's pause for a moment and remember that we are in God's presence at this time.

(pause...)

7 We'll use one of St Patrick's prayers:

Let us pray:

**Christ be with me and within me.
Christ be behind me and before me.
Christ be beside me
    to comfort and restore me.
Christ be below and above me
    in peace and in danger.**

**Christ be within the hearts
    of all who love me.
Christ be in the words
    of friend and stranger.**

✤✤✤✤✤✤✤✤✤✤✤✤✤✤✤✤✤✤✤

📖 *"The Spirit seethed in me," said Patrick, reflecting on being aware of God's presence during his time in the fields.*

📖 *In the book, "The Cry of the Deer", David Adam, the author, reflects on "St Patrick's Breastplate", the prayer of which the above words are the concluding part. It is one of the finest books offering insights into praying. Triangle Press, 0-281-04284-5*

🎵 Christ be beside me; In you my God; I watch the sunrise

1 Tomorrow, 19th March, is the anniversary of the sentencing of six English farmworkers to seven years' transportation in Australia. They are called 'The Tolpuddle Martyrs', after the name of their village in Dorset. Their sentence in 1834 could have resulted in their deaths because of the harsh conditions in the place to which they had been sent. They were sentenced because at that time it was illegal to organise trade union activities in the countryside. Such was the outrage throughout the country that their sentences were cancelled after two years, and they returned to the country as heroes.

2 In 1996, over 150 years later, the Catholic Bishops of England and Wales produced a document called 'The Common Good'. In it, they wrote:

"Work is more than a way of making a living: it is a vocation, a participation in God's creative activity...

3 *"Workers have rights which... include the right to decent work, to just wages, to security of employment, to adequate rest and holidays, to limitation of hours of work, to health and safety protection, to non-discrimination, to form and join trade unions, and, as a last resort, to go on strike."*

4 *Let us pray:*

Lord Jesus,
   lead us to grow in your image
   and become more fully human.
Lead us to respect and value
   all other people
   that we may work together
   for justice for all
   and the building of your kingdom.
Amen.

📖 *The quote is from 'The Common Good' (90,91).*

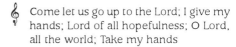 Come let us go up to the Lord; I give my hands; Lord of all hopefulness; O Lord, all the world; Take my hands

19 MARCH

1 Looking at a world map, we see that the islands of Hawaii are in the northern part of the Pacific Ocean. One of that island group is called Molokai. Over a hundred years ago the only people who lived there were lepers. No one was allowed to leave the island; once people arrived, they stayed and died there. No one visited, because it was thought that they would bring back leprosy to those who were well. The lepers' housing, sanitation and medical care were all very inadequate.

2 Father Damien was a priest from Belgium who arrived in Honolulu, the capital of the Hawaiian islands, on this day (the feast of Saint Joseph) in 1864. After a short time, Damien realised that the only thing he could do for the lepers was to go and live with them.

3 At first, the people of Molokai did not know how to take Damien, but eventually many realised that he wanted to be with them, and many felt that they wanted to live as Christians. 20 years after joining the lepers of Molokai, he started his sermon at Sunday Mass with the words: *"My fellow-lepers"*. Wanting to be with the people had cost him his own health: he would die as a leper himself.

4 Let's pray
   for those with the disease of leprosy.
   Let's pray, too,
      for all who are cut off from others,
      for all who are isolated in life,
      and for those whose commitment
      costs them greatly.
   Let's pray for AIDS victims,
      and for all who experience prejudice.

5 **Father,**
   help us to see and love in others
   what you see and love in them.
   Amen.

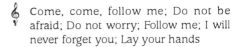
Diana, Princess of Wales, (1/7/61 - 31/8/97) helped to break down barriers by shaking the hands of lepers and of AIDS victims.

Come, come, follow me; Do not be afraid; Do not worry; Follow me; I will never forget you; Lay your hands

(See also 4 January)

1 Today many people use a word-processor to produce letters, essays and documents. If we lose what we've produced, we can always create another copy from the computer disc. Photocopiers, too, are used to provide back-up copies.

2 Many of the world's great writers such as Shakespeare had no easy way of copying or even altering texts - nor did the great scientist, Sir Isaac Newton, who died on this day in 1727.

3 Isaac Newton worked hard and spent some years producing a book. When it was almost finished, he put all his hand-written pages into one pile, and then left the room to get something to eat. After a while he began to smell burning. Rushing back into the room, he saw that his faithful dog, Diamond, had knocked over the candle beside which Newton had been working. Most of the pages of his book were destroyed. What did Newton do? He simply patted his dog, and said: *"Diamond, you don't know what trouble you've caused me, but you know no better."* The following day he started the long process of writing his book all over again.

4 *Let us pray:*

Lord, I pray for gifts and talents
that will help me and other people.
As I pray for these gifts
I know, too,
that I will need to work hard
at developing them
  - to become more patient,
  - to grow in wisdom,
  - and to be faithful in friendship.
May I be as faithful to others
as you are to me.
Amen.

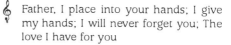

Father, I place into your hands; I give my hands; I will never forget you; The love I have for you

21 MARCH

1 From 1948 until 1990, "apartheid" was the system in South Africa. The word "apartheid" means "separateness", and the laws enforced a very firm separation of people according to race and colour. On this day in 1960 about 15,000 black people formed a peaceful demonstration against the "pass laws" which forced blacks to carry identification and travel permits with them all the time. The police opened fire in the black township of Sharpeville. 56 black people were killed, and a further 162 were wounded. It is known as the 'Sharpeville Massacre'.

2 We remind ourselves of the evils of all systems that declare some people to be inferior because they are "different" in some way. We think of apartheid in South Africa, Nazi rule throughout Europe, Pol Pot in Cambodia, and Stalin in the Soviet Union.

3. *Let us pray:*

Father,
   you have made all people
      in your own likeness,
   and you love all that you have made.
Your Son was born
   as a member of a Jewish family,
   and was recognised
   by wise men from the east.
He rejoiced in the faith
   of a Roman soldier
   and a Syrian woman,
   and he praised Samaritans
   for their attitude and good works.
He welcomed the Greeks
   who searched for him,
   and he was helped to carry his cross
   by an African.

4 Father, may our human family
      not become separated from you
   by building barriers
   of race and colour,
   of class and belief.
Inspire us to recognise
   that we are all made
   in your image and likeness,
   so that we may grow
   in appreciation of all people,
   and encourage each other
   to grow in pride
   in who we are
   and who we are called to be.
May we recognise your Son in our midst,
   and live truly as brothers and sisters.
Amen.

🕮 (3): Gen 1^{27}, Wis 2^{23}, Wis 11^{24}; Lk 2, Mt 2^{1-12}
   Lk 7^{10}, Mk 7^{26}, Lk 17^{19}, Lk 10^{36}
   Jn 12^{20}, Lk 23^{26}

🕮 (4): Jn 11^{52}
   Gen 1^{27}, Wis 2^{23}, Lk 1^{48}, Jn 15^{15}
   Lk 24^{31}, 1 Pet 3^{8}, 1 Jn 4^{20}.

🕮 Acts 10^{1-35} - God has no favourites: anyone of any nationality is acceptable to him.

♪ Amazing grace; Christ is our king; Come let us go up to the Lord

1 The Nazis came to power in Germany in January 1933. From then on, concentration camps were established, and people were put there without trial - Jews, gypsies, disabled people, homosexuals, some prisoners of war, political and religious opponents.

2 On this day - 22nd March - 1933, the Nazis opened a concentration camp called Dachau, near Munich in Germany. By the end of the Second World War, millions had been killed in all the Nazi camps.

3 Despite all the suffering (suffering that we can't even begin to imagine) a prayer was discovered on a piece of wrapping paper beside the body of a dead child in another concentration camp - built at a place called Ravensbruck, where 92,000 women and children were murdered. We don't know who wrote this prayer, but we make it our own today:

4 **O Lord, remember not only**
the men and women of good will,
but also those of ill will.
But do not remember
all the suffering
they have inflicted on us.
Remember instead
the good things that have come to us
thanks to this suffering -
our comradeship, our loyalty,
our humility, our courage,
our generosity,
and the greatness of heart
which have all grown out of this.
And when they come to judgement,
let all the good things
that have come out of this
be their forgiveness.
Amen.

📖 *The prayer needs to be read slowly and with feeling.*

♪ God forgave my sin; Lay your hands; Lord, make me a means; Make me a channel

23 MARCH

(See also 29 February)

1 Tomorrow - 24th March - marks the anniversary in 1603 of the death of one of England's greatest rulers - Queen Elizabeth I. She was desperate for more time to live, and her last words were: *"All my possessions for a moment of time."*

2 *Let us pray that we use our time well:*

Lord,
it is in this place and in this time
that you want me to grow.
You give me the time I need
to live as you want me to live.
Help me to use
my time and opportunities wisely.
Help me to value and treasure
all the people you put into my life,
and lead me to live in thankfulness.
Amen.

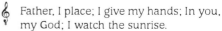 Father, I place; I give my hands; In you, my God; I watch the sunrise.

1 On 24th March 1980, Archbishop Oscar Romero was celebrating Mass in his cathedral when he was shot dead. He was archbishop of San Salvador, the capital of El Salvador, a country in Central America - ruled by an extreme right-wing government, backed by the army, and well-known for repressing and torturing and murdering its citizens.

2 Six days later, on 30th March, thousands attended Archbishop Romero's funeral, gathering in the square in front of the cathedral. Even there, at the funeral of the murdered Archbishop, 20 people were shot dead by the army, despite the international news media who were present to report whatever they saw.

3 *Let us pray:*

Lord, we bring before you
all who are imprisoned unjustly
and all who are tortured.
We think of those people who live in fear
of injustice and repression.
We pray that the minds of those
who abuse others
may be turned
to what is good and honourable.
May those of us who live in freedom
not take our heritage for granted,
but be of good influence
in leading others
to value one another
as brothers and sisters.
Amen.

📖 *John 15[13] - a man can have no greater love than to lay down his life for his friends.*

📖 *See 24 January for mention of letter-writing campaigns with 'Amnesty International'.*

🎼 Come, let us go up; O Lord all the world;
This is what Yahweh asks of you

1   Today, 9 months before 25th December, we mark the feast of the Annunciation - when the angel visited Mary, announcing that she was to be the mother of Jesus: *"You will conceive and bear a son, and you must name him 'Jesus'. He will be the Son of God."*

2   Mary asked the angel: *"I am a virgin, so how can this come about?" "The Holy Spirit will cause you to conceive,"* the angel told her. And Mary replied: *"Fulfil in me, Lord, all that you have said."*

3   We'll use Mary's response as our prayer today.
Let us pray:

Fulfil in me, Lord, all that you have said.

4   Jesus said: *Come to me, all you who have heavy burdens, and I will give you rest. Peace is what I leave with you - my own peace. Do not be worried or upset; do not be afraid.*
Let us pray:

Fulfil in me, Lord, all that you have said.

5   Jesus said: *Be healed; get up and walk; unbind him; your sins are forgiven; be clean; go in peace and be healed of your trouble.*
Let us pray:

Fulfil in me, Lord, all that you have said.

6   Jesus said: *I do not call you servants; I call you friends. As I have loved you, so you must love one another. When two or three come together in my name, I will be amongst them.*
Let us pray:

Fulfil in me, Lord, all that you have said.

7   Jesus said: *I will ask the Father, and he will give you another helper - the Holy Spirit, to be with you for ever.*
Let us pray:

Fulfil in me, Lord, all that you have said.

8   Jesus said: *I am the vine and you are the branches. Those who remain in me, and I in them, will bear much fruit. I have come that you may have life, life in all its fullness.*
Let us pray:

Fulfil in me, Lord, all that you have said.

(4) = Mt 11^{28};Jn 14^{27}
(5) = Mt 9^{29};Jn 5^{8};Jn 11^{44};Mk 2^{5};Mk 1^{41},Mk 5^{34}
(6) = Jn 15^{15};Jn 13^{34},Mt 18^{20}
(7) = Jn 14^{16}
(8) = Jn 15^{5};Jn 10^{10}

Luke $1^{26-38ff}$: the Annunciation.

Hail Mary; Holy Virgin by God's decree;
The Angel Gabriel

1 The Cardinal-Archbishop of Paris was celebrating Mass with two priest-friends in the great Cathedral of Notre Dame in the French capital.

2 In his sermon, the Cardinal mentioned a true story. Three teenage lads agreed that, for a laugh, they would go into a church, and go to the priest for the Sacrament of Reconciliation ('Confession'). The three lads agreed that each would make up a list of sins to mention.

3 So the first lad went in, and said: *"Father, I've robbed a bank."* The second lad went in and said: *"I've killed somebody."* When it was the turn of the third lad, he tried not to laugh, and said: *"I've robbed a bank **and** killed somebody."* The priest - knowing, of course, what was happening - said to the third lad: *"For your penance I want you to go and stand in front of the big crucifix in church, and I want you to say some words that I'll give you. Say them three times, and say them in a loud voice."*

4 And so the lad came out of the confessional and laughed with his friends. He went to the front and stood before the large crucifix - they were still laughing at what had happened. And then the lad repeated - still for a laugh - the words that he'd been told to say: *"Jesus, you died for me, and I don't give a damn."* The second time, he said the words a little more loudly. The third time he found himself saying the words more slowly, and something he couldn't explain happened within, and he discovered that the words became a question to himself: *"Jesus, you died for me, and I don't give a damn (?)"*

5 The Cardinal - telling this story in his sermon - continued. He said to the people in the cathedral: *"I told you that this* *was a true story. How do I know? Those two lads from years ago are sitting with me now - they are the two priests who are celebrating Mass with me. And I **also** know this is true because **I** am that third boy. I was the one who spoke before the crucifix."*

6 *Let's spend a moment in silence, praying very honestly, as we say a few words to Jesus...*

(pause...)

🔊 *A crucifix or an icon could be in a prominent place.*

🎵 Do not worry; Father, in my life I see; Follow me; God forgave my sin; O Lord all the world; Though the mountains may fall

27 MARCH

1 It is the anniversary today in 1898 of the first international transmission of a radio message. It was sent by Marconi across the English Channel - from France to England. The message was to 'The Times' newspaper from a correspondent in northern France. This was the message that was broadcast:

2 "Communication between England and the Continent was set up yesterday morning by the Marconi system of wireless telegraphy.... Signor Marconi is here conducting the trials and is very satisfied with the results."

3 Let us pray:

We know, Lord,
   that there are many radio waves
   travelling through this room
      at the moment,
   but we need a radio
   to be able to tune in
   to the different frequencies.
Isn't it a bit like that with prayer, Lord,
   "tuning in" to your presence with us?

4 We remember that you said
   that you would be with us,
   so we do know in our minds
   that you are present.
But there's a difference
   between *knowing* that you're present
   and *growing in the faith*
   that you are beside us.
We ask for the power of your Spirit
   in our lives each day,
   so that we may live more fully
   in your presence.
Only then will our attitude
   and words and actions
   better reflect yours.
Amen.

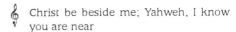 Guglielmo Marchese Marconi was born in Italy in 1874, and died in 1937.

Christ be beside me; Yahweh, I know you are near

1 Today marks the birthday in the year 1515 of St Teresa of Avila, in Spain. She wrote:

2 *Christ has no body on earth now but ours:*
   no hands but ours, no feet but ours.
Ours are the eyes
   through which Christ's compassion
   is to look upon the world.
Ours are the feet
   with which he is to go about doing good.
Ours are the hands
   with which he is to bless others now.

3 *Let us pray:*

Lord Jesus,
I give you my hands
   - to do your work.
I give you my feet
   - to go your way.
I give you my eyes
   - to see as you do.
I give you my tongue
   - to speak your words.
I give you my mind
   - that you may think in me.
I give you my spirit
   - that you may pray in me.
Above all, I give you my heart
   that you may love, in me,
   your Father and all mankind.
I give you my whole self
   that you may grow in me,
   so that it is you, Lord Jesus,
   who live and work and pray in me.
Amen.

Grail Prayer

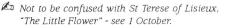

Not to be confused with St Terese of Lisieux, "The Little Flower" - see 1 October.

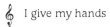 I give my hands

1 In every World Cup football match since the 1980s, two people could be seen behind one of the goals. When the cameras focused on the goalmouth they held up a small sign which simply read:

Jn 3:16

2 A number of people who were in the crowd, and many watching TV in many countries throughout the world, realised that this meant:

St John's Gospel, Chapter 3, verse 16.

3 Some of the people who saw "Jn 3:16" looked it up in the Bible, and realised that the words were appropriate for an event that was being watched around the world. This is what the passage from St John's Gospel says:

4 *"God loved the world so much*
that he gave his only Son,
so that everyone who believes in him
may not be lost,
but may have eternal life."

5 The same passage appears in all the many languages in which the Bible has been translated.

6 *In French:*

Car Dieu a tant aimé le monde
qu'il a donné son Fils unique,
afin que quiconque croit en lui ne se
perde pas,
mais ait la vie éternelle.

7 *In German:*

Denn so lebte Gott die Welt,
dass er seinen eingeborenen Sohn hingab,
damit jeder,
der an ihn glaubt, nicht verlorengehe,
sondern ewiges Leben habe.

8 *In Italian:*

Dio ha tanto amato il mondo
da dare il suo unico Figlio
perché chi crede in lui non muoia
ma abbia vita eterna.

9 *In Spanish:*

Porque tanto am–Dios al mundo
que dio a su Hijo único,
para que todo el que crea en él no perezca
sino que tenga vida eterna.

10 *In Welsh:*

Do, carodd Duw y byd gymaint ned iddo
roi ei unig Fab, er mwyn; bob un sy'n
credu ynddo ef beidio â mynol i ddistryw
ond cael bywyd tragwyddol.

11. *Let us pray:*

God our Father,
  your love for our world
  and for each of us individually
  is so great
  that you sent Jesus, your Son,
  to live fully as one of us.
May he lead us to live in peace
  and work well with each other
  to build your kingdom
  in our world which you love so much.
May your Spirit unite us
  and lead us to appreciate and value
  all who are different from ourselves.
Amen.

Christ is our king; Come let us go up to the Lord; This is what Yahweh asks of you

1 Sunday is the holy day and rest day of Christians. Friday is the day for Moslems. Saturday is the holy day and rest day for Jews. The Jewish Sabbath (the word means 'rest') starts the evening before, because days are counted from sunset to sunset.

2 Each Friday evening, then, there is a prayer service in the synagogue, the Jewish place of worship. Afterwards members of the family gather together at home. It is always the mother who starts the sabbath prayers by saying a blessing over the two candles that are used. Her husband and children gather round her and she prays:

> "Blessed are you, Lord our God,
> King of the Universe.
> You have made us holy
> by your commandments,
> and you have instructed us
> to kindle the Sabbath light."

3 A passage is read from the Scriptures. Then the family sit down for their Sabbath meal. The father recites a blessing (called the 'Kiddush'), and he blesses a cup of wine:

> "Blessed are you, Lord our God.
> You create the fruit of the vine."

He blesses the bread:

> "Blessed are you, Lord our God.
> You bring forth bread from the earth."

4 As we are about to use the same words of blessing that Jewish families use every Friday evening, let us pray for a blessing on all whom we love and care for:

5 Let us pray:

May the Lord bless you and keep you. May the Lord shine his face upon you. May he show you his loving kindness and bring you peace. Amen.

(Numbers 6²⁴)

❖❖❖❖❖❖❖❖❖❖❖❖❖❖❖❖❖❖

📖 *These "Blessed-are-you" prayers are the basis for the Offertory prayers in the Roman Catholic Mass.*

📖 *As the Jewish sabbath starts the evening before, so the Roman Catholic Church celebrates Sunday Mass on Saturday evenings as well as on the Sunday itself.*

 Father, I place; May the blessing of God

31 MARCH

1 On the 31st March in 1855, the author Charlotte Brontë died, aged 39. She had lived in Yorkshire. In one of her books, 'Jane Eyre', she wrote:

2 *"We know that God is everywhere,*
but certainly we feel his presence most
when his works are on the grandest scale
spread before us,
and it is in the unclouded night-sky,
where his worlds wheel their silent course,
that we read clearest his infinitude,
his omnipotence, his omnipresence."

3 We can think, as well, of one of the great saints, Ignatius Loyola, who could not look at the stars in the night sky without being moved to tears by God's beauty.

4 *Let us pray:*

God our Father, open our eyes
to the beauty of your creation.
Inspire us to appreciate
all the wonders of life.
May all that we see lead us to you.
Amen.

 Christ be beside me; O Lord my God, the Father of creation; Yahweh, I know you are near

(See also 3, 12, 14 July)

1 William Harvey, who died on this day in 1578, was a doctor in London. He is recognised as having been the first to discover that blood circulates around the body, pumped by the beat of the heart.

2 Our prayer today has been used by some people with heart problems. The prayer refers to the "pounding of the heart", and the need for us all to slow down and appreciate what is around us:

3 *Let us pray:*

Slow me down, Lord!
Ease the pounding of my heart
  by the quietening and calming
    of my mind.
Break the tensions
  of my nerves and muscles
  with the soothing music
  of the singing streams
  that live in my memory.
Give me, amidst the confusion
    of the day,
  the calmness of the everlasting hills.
Steady my hurried pace
  with a vision
    of your eternal reach of time,
  and restore and heal me
    in the hours of sleep.

4 Teach me the art
  of appreciating what is ordinary:
  of slowing down
  to look at and become more aware
    of the beauty around me;
  to take time to be with others,
  to sit and enjoy music
    or a good book
  - to give myself time for myself.

5 Remind me each day
  of the fable
    of the hare and the tortoise,
  that I may know
  that the race is not always
    to the swift;
  that there is more to life
  than increasing its speed.

6 Let me look upwards
  into the branches
    of the towering trees
  and know
  that they grew great and strong
  because they grew slowly and well.
Slow me down, Lord,
  and inspire me to send my roots
  deep into the soil
    of life's enduring values.
Slow me down, Lord,
  that I may grow true and well
    in your light.
Amen.

📖 The prayer is attributed to Cardinal Cushing of the USA.

📖 See also 3, 12, 14 July

📖 Ecclesiastes $3^{1\text{-}13}$ - "a time for everything".

📖 Mark Twain, regarding April Fool's Day, wrote: "This is the day upon which we are reminded of what we are on the other 364 days!".

🎼 Be still and know I am with you; Give me joy in my heart; This day God gives me; Yahweh, I know you are near

2 APRIL

1 Let's pause for a moment to call to mind that we are in God's presence.

(pause...)

2 An English saint called Richard of Chichester (whose feastday it is tomorrow) wrote a short prayer that can easily be memorised and used quietly at different times throughout the day. The words of his prayer have been set to music, and the song 'Day by day' is found on the album of the musical, 'Godspel'. We use his words as our prayer today:

3 *Let us pray:*

Jesus, Friend and Brother,
   may we know you more clearly,
   love you more dearly,
   and follow you more nearly,
   day by day.

✍ *This is the kind of short prayer that some people choose to memorise and then use from time to time.*

✍ *Tomorrow, 3rd April, is the anniversary in 1253 of the death of St Richard of Chichester.*

🎵 Christ be beside me; I will be with you; I watch the sunrise; In you, my God; Do not be afraid; Follow me; If I am lacking love.

APRIL 3

1 Late one evening, Percy Shaw was driving through the countryside by car from Bradford to Halifax in Yorkshire. There were no lights along the road. Suddenly the light from his headlights was reflected back to him from the eyes of a cat, sitting on a fence. Without that cat he would not have realised there was a bend in the road, and would have driven into the fence, and probably down the steep hillside beyond. The reflection from the cat's eyes saved him from serious injury or from death.

2 Could he make use of what happened to him to benefit others? He spent a year trying to invent something that could guide drivers in the dark and in the fog. He set two glass prisms back-to-back in a rubber base, each with a mirror made of aluminium. They were good at reflecting a car's own light back to the driver.

3 His "cat's eyes" (as he called them) soon became dirty in the middle of the road, and he realised that, if they were still to reflect light back, somehow they would have to clean themselves. He added a spring to the rubber base of each glass prism. When cars ran over the "cat's eyes", now they would be pressed down against a rubber pad, and so be wiped clean

4 On this day in 1934 Percy Shaw laid the first set of fifty "cat's eyes" (at his own expense) along a stretch of road near Bradford that had a bad reputation for accidents. Once the Ministry of Transport realised that the number of accidents there dropped considerably, they approved his idea.

5 Percy Shaw's invention - still called "cat's eyes" - have saved the lives of many, and have made it much easier and safer to drive cars. Percy Shaw had seen that something needed to be done, and got on with it.

6 *Let us pray:*

Lord, we ask
 that we may have the vision
 to see when something is not right
 and then try to do something
  about it:
 - that we may notice
 when someone is unhappy
  or isn't well,
 and set out to encourage them;
 - that we may notice
 when someone feels left out,
 and then do what we can
 to help them feel part of things;
 - that we may notice
 when something needs to be done,
 and then get on with it.
Lord, we ask that we may notice
 all that is around us,
 and live in a positive
  and cheerful way.
Amen.

❖❖❖❖❖❖❖❖❖❖❖❖❖❖❖❖❖❖❖❖

 *Percy Shaw became a millionaire because of his invention, but he lived in a simple manner for the rest of his life.*

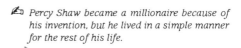 Walk with me, O my Lord; The light of Christ; Shine on me; Be still and know I am with you; Father, I place into your hands

115

4 APRIL

(See also 15 January and 5 April)

1 In the United States of the 1960's, people were still segregated (separated) according to their colour. Those of other colour were kept at a distance from whites. Only whites could sit at the front of buses. In restaurants and cafes, people were kept apart according to colour. There were white-only schools. Most blacks were not allowed to vote.

2 Martin Luther King was a Baptist minister. He became involved in trying to get people to change their attitude of hatred and prejudice. He always preached non-violence despite the threats, bombings, stabbings and other violence that was done to him. On this day in 1968, Martin Luther King was shot dead.

3 One of his best-known speeches was delivered at the largest rally ever held in the United States - when a quarter of a million people gathered in Washington in a Civil Rights demonstration. He said:

4 *"I have a dream*
that one day on the red hills of Georgia
sons of former slaves
and the sons of former slave-owners
will be able to sit down together
at the table of brotherhood.
I have a dream
that my four little children
will one day live in a nation
where they will not be judged
by the colour of their skin
but by the content of their character.
I have a dream today."

5 *Let us pray:*

Father, sometimes I am too quick
  to draw conclusions
    about other people,
  and I fail to see
  many of the qualities in individuals.

Remove from me any prejudices
  that might lead me
    to think of myself
  as "better" than someone else.
If anyone should be negative
  towards me,
  inspire me to remain positive
    towards them.
Because we are all different,
  there are many things
  I need to learn from others,
  and so I ask for the gifts
  of understanding and wisdom
  and a clear vision
  that will lead me to treat others
  as I would like them to treat me.
Amen.

6 Let's each of us think of two people in our lives at home or in school or work today whom we need to value and respect a little more. In silence, let's think of ways today in which we can improve those relationships.

(pause...)

📖 *Joel 3¹ - "Your old men shall dream dreams, and your young men shall have visions; Isaiah 61 & Luke 4$^{16-22}$ - Set free the captives; John 11^{52} - Jesus died to bring together all God's people scattered far and wide; Acts 10¹-11^{18} - "God has no favourites; anyone of any nationality, is acceptable to him.".*

🎼 The love/dream I have for you; God's Spirit is in my heart; Christ is our king; All that I am/dream; Oh Lord all the world belongs to you; Follow me

APRIL 5

(See also 15 January and 4 April)

1 We are going to listen to part of a sermon preached by Martin Luther King, two months before he was assassinated on 4th April 1968. A tape recording of him preaching that sermon was played at his own funeral. These were his words, played back for everyone to hear:

2 *"Every now and then I think about my own death, and I think about my own funeral. If any of you are around when I have to meet my day, I don't want a long funeral. And if you get somebody to deliver the eulogy, tell them not to talk too long. Every now and then I wonder what I want them to say. Tell them not to mention that I have a Nobel Peace Prize - that isn't important. Tell them not to mention that I have three or four hundred other awards - that's not important.*

3 *I'd like somebody to mention that day, that Martin Luther King tried to give his life serving others. I'd like for somebody to say that day, that "Martin Luther King tried to love somebody." I want you to say that day, that I "did try to feed the hungry; that I did try, in my life, to visit those who were in prison." I want you to say that I "tried to love and serve humanity." I won't have any money to leave behind. I won't have the fine and luxurious things of life to leave behind. But I just want to leave a committed life behind."*

4 Our response to the prayers will be: *"hear our prayer."*
Hear our prayer.

5 Let us pray that we may discover what is really important in life.
Lord, in your mercy - hear our prayer.

6 Let us pray that we may respect and value each person who comes into our lives.
Lord, in your mercy - hear our prayer.

7 Let us pray that we may be willing to learn from others.
Lord, in your mercy - hear our prayer.

8 Let us pray for those who will experience hatred, abuse, and violence this day.
Lord, in your mercy - hear our prayer.

9 Let us pray for people of violence, that their attitude and behaviour may change.
Lord, in your mercy - hear our prayer.

📖 *"eulogy" - some words about the life of the person who has died.*

📖 *Do you agree with Martin Luther King's statement that "If a man hasn't discovered something he would die for, he isn't fit to live"?*

📖 *Mt 25³¹⁻³⁶ - visit me in prison, when sick; feed the hungry.*

🎼 Whatsoever you do; There is a world where people; The love/dream I have for you; O Lord all the world; Christ is our king; Follow me

117

6 APRIL

1 The first recorded Olympic Games took place in the year 776 BC, although they may have been held for a few hundred years before that time. The Games were held every four years at Olympus, the place where the father of the Greek gods, Zeus, was thought to live. Invitations went out to many cities throughout the Greek world, inviting them to send athletes. In the year 394 A.D. the Roman Emperor no longer allowed the Games to continue.

2 Just over 1500 years later, on this day in 1896, the first of the modern-day Olympic Games was opened. The Games were the idea of the French sportsman, Baron Pierre de Coubertin, who hoped they would encourage many to think of physical fitness, as well as helping to promote understanding and respect between nations. His ideal was that nations would compete on the playing field rather than on the battlefield.

3 In those first Olympics of modern days in 1896, 13 countries took part, with 285 athletes. In our own days about 11,000 athletes attend from 180 countries.

4 The Olympic Flag dates from 1913. The 5 connected rings are of different colours, representing the 5 continents. The flag of every country shares at least one colour with the Olympic rings.

5 Some words of Baron de Coubertin are often quoted at the Games:
"The important thing in the Olympic Games is not winning, but taking part. The essential thing in life is not conquering but fighting well."

6 *Let us pray:*

**Lord, inspire me to give of my best
and make good use
of the talents you have given me.
Show me how to be positive in attitude,
appreciating and valuing others,
always being ready to encourage
and give praise.
Sometimes I draw conclusions
about people
in terms of what I think
is meant by "success" and "failure",
but the "failure" of one person
might count as a great "success"
of someone with other talents.
Lead me never to judge people
but to accept others as they are,
knowing that it is together,
each with our differences,
that we build up your Kingdom.
Amen.**

📖 *see also 29 May (4-6) and 23 July.*

📖 *Coubertin was buried in Lausanne, Switzerland but, as he requested in his will, his heart was buried at Olympia in Greece.*

📖 *The music by Vangelis of 'Chariots of Fire' could be played. The film of that name is of the 1924 Olympics, held in Paris.*

📖 *Phil 3[14]:* "I am racing for the finish".

   2 Tim 4[5-8]: "fought the good fight, run the race to the finish, won the crown".

📖 *For "success" and "failure" see also 4 March, 29 May*

𝄞 Come, let us go up to the Lord

1 Let's pause for a moment to remind ourselves that we are in God's presence...

(pause...)

2 John Baptist De La Salle is the patron saint of teachers, and today is the anniversary of his death. 300 years ago he wrote these words for teachers:

3 *"Take even more care
of the young people entrusted to you
than if they were the children of a king."*

4 His words remind all of us of whatever age to respect one another's dignity as unique individuals.

5 A few years ago, a black South African teacher talked of working with black South African schoolchildren. He had spoken to one lad who looked miserable, and said to him:

"You are created in the image of God. Don't walk round with your eyes cast down."

It has been said that the job of a Christian school is **not** to make people into something that they are not, but to convince them of who they already are.

6 "Respect" is about treating others in the same way that we would like to be treated. Let's each of us focus on **one** way today of showing respect for others in school.

For example,
- using the person's name when speaking to them;
- holding the door open for whoever is behind us;
- saying "thanks" whenever someone gives us a book or a piece of paper, and when we get our meal in the dining room.

7 Let's pause for a moment and think of **one** practical way today of showing our respect for others...

(pause...)

8 *Let us pray:*

Lord Jesus,
you invite each of us by name
and you call us "friends".
Lead us to show
as much respect and care for others
as we would like them to show for us.
Help us to look for
and bring out the best
in all who share our lives this day.
Amen.

🖎 *Could ask for other examples of showing respect and care for others in school, and then put together a list. One point could be displayed on the classroom wall each week, or a set of three could be considered the "Action Plan" of the class for a term.*

🖎 *The interview with the South African teacher was shown on 'Songs of Praise', 4/12/94.*

🖎 *"I call you friends" - John 15¹⁴⁻¹⁵.*

🖎 *John Baptist De La Salle was born in Rheims, France, 30/4/1651, and died on 7/4/1719. He was declared the Patron Saint of teachers in 1950. Some details about his life and inspiration may be obtained by writing to the author.*

🖎 *See also 15 May..*

♪ Here I am, Lord; I give my hands; Take my hands

8 APRIL

1 We are going to listen to a letter written by a teenager to Brother John, a friend whom she had come to know:

2 *Dear Brother John,*
If you like, you can tear this letter up and never read it. I just needed to put my feelings down.
I learned today that someone I went to junior school with has died. Just like that! He was only fifteen, with nothing apparently wrong with him. He had a brain haemorrhage. I just couldn't believe it. Why, oh why, did he die? He was only 15 - his life was just beginning. He always used to talk about the future - now he has no future. I remember a happy boy, always smiling, very rarely crying! Then I think of him cold and lifeless, and it hurts. How much more it must hurt his family - God forgive me for being so selfish!
But why did God take him away? Why take such a youthful person? Why not take someone who is in great pain or suffers in other ways? Not him. I shall never even begin to understand God. People say he always acts for the best - yet how can my friend's death be for the best? I know I can pray for him, and though I believe he's in Heaven, how can I ever be sure?
Oh God, this sounds rather as though I don't believe in you. I'm sorry, but I still feel rather shocked.
Dear John, if you read this, please pray for my friend. If not, never mind, just writing it helped a little.
Love,
Susan.

3 Let's pray in silence for a moment for those who, today, will suffer the death of someone they love dearly...
(pause...)

4 Let's pray in silence for a moment that, as others will help us in **our** times of difficulty, we, too, will be ready to stand with others in **their** difficulties....
(pause...)

5 *Let us pray:*

Loving Father,
  to you the dead do not die
  and, in death, our life is changed
  - not ended.
We believe
  that all that binds us together
  in love and friendship
  does not end with death.
Hear our prayers for those close to us
  who have died.
As you have made each of them
  in your image and likeness
  and have called them by name,
  hold them safe in your love
  in your kingdom
  of light, happiness and peace.
Your Son told us
  that those who mourn are "blessed",
  because only those
  who love greatly can mourn.
Bless us this day
  with the warmth of your love
  as we mourn those we have lost.
Amen.

✣✣✣✣✣✣✣✣✣✣✣✣✣✣✣✣✣

✍ *The letter was written to Brother John, who was then a member of the community of De La Salle Brothers working in St Cassian's Retreat Centre, Kintbury, Berkshire.)*

✍ *Particular sensitivity may be required if a relative or friend of someone present has died recently.*

 Do not be afraid; Abide with me; Christ be beside me; There is a world; Make me a channel of your peace

(See also 4 March)

1 In 1861 Abraham Lincoln was elected 16th President of the United States, just as the country was about to break up in Civil War for four years between the States of the North and those of the South.

2 One of the reasons for the start of the Civil War lay in the fact that the South had slavery. Of the 9 million people in the South, 4 million were slaves. Lincoln said:

   " 'A house divided against itself
   cannot stand.'
   I believe this government
   cannot endure permanently,
   half slave and half free."

   He abolished slavery, declaring all people to be free.

3 During the Civil War, 4 out of every 100 Americans were either killed or seriously wounded. Of every 100 soldiers, 5 died in battle and 20 died of illness and disease.

4 Today is the anniversary of the end of the American Civil War in 1865.

5 Abraham Lincoln wrote a prayer about injustice and war and all who suffer in war. We use Lincoln's words today, as we pray for those who need justice and healing and peace in their lives:

6 **Grant, O merciful God,**
   that with malice toward none,
   with charity to all,
   with firmness in the right
   as you give us to see the right,
   we may strive to finish
      the work we are in:
   to bind up the nation's wounds,
   to care for those
      who have borne the battle

and for their widows and orphans,
to do all which may achieve and cherish
a just and lasting peace
among ourselves and with all nations.
Amen.

✐ *We can pray for all countries where there is war or civil strife.*

✐ *Abraham Lincoln: 12/2/1809-15/5/1865. The prayer is an extract from Lincoln's Second Inaugural Speech.*

✐ *From a nation then of 35 million people, some 620,000 men were killed during the American Civil War.*

✐ *"Set free the captives" - Isaiah 61 & Luke $4^{16\text{-}22}$; cheating the poor - Amos 5^{24},$8^{4\text{-}6}$*

♪ Come, let us go up to the Lord; Make me a channel of your peace; Lord, make me a means of your peace; God's Spirit is in my heart

10 APRIL

1 Fruit and vegetables from many countries around the world are found in our shops each day. Bananas first appeared in British shops on this day in the year 1633.

2 Today, out of every £1 we pay for some **bananas**, only 11 pence goes to those who have grown and picked them in far-away countries. The other 89 pence goes to all the 'middlemen' - those who pack and transport the fruit to Britain, and to the big retailers and the shops.

3 With most jars of **coffee** that we buy, 92 pence out of every pound that we spend goes to all the middlemen - including those who export and process the coffee beans, and those who package the jars and sell them. Out of every pound that we spend on jars of coffee, only 8 pence goes to those who grow the coffee.

4 More and more people are trying to be sure that workers in far-away countries are paid fairly for the goods that come to us. The "Fairtrade Foundation" was set up in 1992 by Christian Aid, Oxfam, and CAFOD (the Catholic Fund for Overseas Development). "Fairtrade" products include tea, coffee and chocolate, and they are to be found in most major supermarkets, with a "Fairtrade" label on them. The "Fairtrade" label guarantees that checks have been made to ensure fair wages, decent working conditions, good health and safety standards, and long-term contracts. Coffee from "Fairtrade" is also available in the House of Commons.

5 Let's simply spend a few moments in silence, reflecting on how wealthy we are, compared with the majority of people throughout the world...

(pause...)

6 *Let us pray:*

Lord, that we may live simply so that others may simply live.

📖 *The Fairtrade Foundation, 7th Floor, Regent House, 89 Kingsway, London WC2 6RH.*

📖 *'The Independent' newspaper of 13/11/97 carried a photo of the Speaker of the House of Commons lending her support at the official launch of Fairtrade coffee in the House.*

 O Lord all the world belongs to you

1 Apollo 13 was to have been the third manned landing on the Moon, and it blasted off from Cape Kennedy on this day in 1970. Two days into the journey, a major explosion took place in the oxygen tanks. Electrical power was lost in the main part of the ship (the Command Module), and the three astronauts had to move into the small cone. This was the Lunar Module which would have been the only part to land on the Moon, and would later have blasted off to rejoin the Command Module for the return journey to Earth.

2 Because of the explosion, there was no question of landing on the Moon; the only hope was to return the three men safely.

3 The spacecraft travelled round the far side of the Moon, gaining speed from the Moon's gravity, propelling the craft back to Earth. With very little energy remaining for the essential powering of the computer, the heat had to be cut off. One of the men became very ill but, against all odds, the three astronauts were returned safely to Earth.

4 These events are recorded in the film, *"Apollo 13"*, starring Tom Hanks as Commander Lovell.

5 Once the craft had travelled round the Moon and then faced towards Earth, Commander Lovell looked out of the window, and held out his thumb to 'cover' the Earth. Reflecting later, he said: *"I could put everything I knew behind my thumb. It gives me a humble feeling of how insignificant we really are in our solar system."*

6 *Let us pray:*

God our Father,
  amidst the vastness of space
  you treasure mankind
  and you call each of us by name.
You so love our world
  that, in the fullness of time,
  you sent Jesus, your Son,
  to live among us.
Inspire us each day
  to live in wonder and appreciation
  of all that is around us,
  and may your love,
  seen fully in Jesus, your Son,
  surround us this day and for ever.
Amen.

✍ *Could use Psalm 8 [as for 12 April] or the prayer for 8 January.*

✍ *The three astronauts were Commander Lovell, Fred Haise, and John Swigert. "Houston, we have a problem" are the often-quoted words of Commander Lovell as he, in a matter-of-fact way, told the Command Centre in Houston, Texas, of the explosion.*

♩ Christ be beside me; O Lord, my God, when I in awesome wonder; Yahweh, I know you are near

12 APRIL

1 On April 12th 1961, a Russian, Yuri Gagarin, became the first person to travel in space. His spacecraft, 'Vostok 1', made a journey of 1 hour 48 minutes, making a single orbit of earth. He was travelling at 17,000 miles per hour (*27,400 km/hr*).

2 When he returned to earth, he reported that he had not seen God in the heavens, referring to people who tend to look upwards when praying to God. Later, a Russian priest said: *"If you haven't seen God on earth, you will never see him in heaven."*

3 Some other astronauts since Yuri Gagarin have found the experience of being in space to lead them closer to God.

4 There are poems in the Bible that reflect on our place in the universe, and we use one of them as our prayer today. It is called 'Psalm 8', and a copy of this psalm was later left on the moon in a sealed capsule by American astronauts:

5 *Let us pray:*

Lord, our God and King,
your greatness is seen
throughout the earth.

6 **When I gaze at the heavens**
which your fingers have formed,
and look at the moon and the stars
which you have set there,
I realise how small we are
in the majesty of your creation.

7 **Yet you treasure us**
above all that you have made,
and you give us control
over all the works of your hand
- animals both wild and tame,
birds in the air,
and the creatures of the sea.

8 **Lord, our God and King,**
your greatness is seen
throughout the earth.

(Psalm 8, paraphrased)

📖 *What might the Russian priest have meant when he said: "If you haven't seen God on earth, you will never see him in heaven" ?*

📖 *Why might some astronauts have felt that their experiences led them closer to God?*

📖 *James Weldon Johnson has an interesting poem, 'The Creation': "And God stepped out on space."*

📖 *Yuri Gagarin, once the most famous person in the world, died in 1968, aged 34, when testing a new aircraft.*

📖 *Psalm 139$^{7-10}$ - "If I climb the heavens you are there*

🎼 O Lord, my God, when I in awesome wonder; This day God gives me; Christ be beside me; Yahweh, I know you are near

1 Comets travel in long stretched-out orbits from near the sun to far out in our solar system of planets, and then back round again towards the sun, gathering speed as the sun's gravity attracts them. One of the most famous comets is called Halley's Comet, which returns every 76 years, last appearing in 1986.

2 Comets are like "dirty snowballs" - they are made of rock, ice and other frozen materials. As a comet approaches the sun, the heat of the sun causes some of it to become vapour and dust that then form frozen particles, stretching millions of miles into the deep cold of space - forming what is called the "tail" of the comet.

3 One of the brightest comets of the last 500 years is named after the two men who discovered it in 1995 - Alan Hale and Thomas Bopp. The Hale-Bopp Comet is 25 miles *(40 km)* in diameter. It was seen from Earth in spring, 1997. Some cities decided to turn down the brightness of their street lights on certain nights, so that the comet could be seen better.

4 The closest the Hale-Bopp Comet ever comes to Earth is 122 million miles. Being so far away, the comet - when viewed from Earth in 1997 - didn't appear to move. When nearest the sun, the comet travels at 98,000 miles per hour. It is now hurtling away from the sun, back into deep space. The tail of the Hale-Bopp Comet varies between 20-60 million miles in length!

5 *Let us pray:*

God our Father,
   may all that we see and experience
   lead us to grow
   in wonder and respect,
that we may value and be thankful
for everything in our lives each day.
Inspire us to choose wisely
   and live positively,
   and make good use
   of our knowledge and talents,
   both for ourselves
   and for the benefit of others.
Amen.

✥✥✥✥✥✥✥✥✥✥✥✥✥✥✥✥✥✥✥

✍ *The closest the comet comes to Earth is 122 million miles. In comparison, the distance between the earth and the sun is 93 million miles. The Hale-Bopp Comet slows down to 250 mph when it is furthest from the sun.*

✍ *"You will shine in the world like bright stars."* *- Phil 2[16]*

🎼 Oh Lord my God, the Father of creation; O Lord, my God, when I in awesome wonder; I watch the sunrise; Yahweh, I know you are near; Laudato sii

14 APRIL

1 One of the greatest ships of its time, the luxury liner the Titanic, set sail on its maiden voyage from Southampton to New York. Just before midnight on 14th April 1912, the Titanic struck an iceberg.

2 The ship had been called "unsinkable" because it had been fitted with water-tight compartments, but more of these were gashed by the iceberg than it was ever thought could be involved in an accident. The huge "unsinkable" ship sank within 3 hours. There were not enough lifeboats for everyone on board. Of about 2,200 people on board, over 1500 died.

3 Investigations after the tragedy showed that the ship had been travelling too fast in an area that sometimes had icebergs. A nearby ship, the Californian, didn't go to the rescue because its radio-operator was off-duty and asleep and so missed the S.O.S. Morse Code messages.

4 Many changes were made because of this tragedy: there was to be someone at the radio 24 hours a day whilst a ship was at sea; there were to be enough life-boats on ships to hold everyone; there were to be lifeboat drills; and there was to be an international patrol to keep watch on icebergs.

5 There have been several films about the sinking of the Titanic. Many think this is one of the worst disasters of all time, especially since human pride and many mistakes led up to the tragedy.

6 Let's pray in silence for all who are suffering...

(pause...)

7 Let's pray for those who care for people who have suffered tragedies in their lives...

(pause...)

8 Let's pray for courage when we will face difficult times...

(pause...)

9 Let's pray for those who place their own safety at risk for the good of others - for all members of the rescue services....

(pause...)

🖾 *What "human pride" might have led up to the tragedy?*

🖾 *The S.O.S. message in Morse Code is three dots, three dashes, and then three dots again.*

🖾 *The wreck of the ship, 2 miles deep, was discovered and photographed in 1985. Since then some items brought up from the wreck have been sold. In 1997 a book was printed, called "Last Dinner of the Titanic", inviting cooks to re-create meals that had been included on the Titanic's menu. Are such things acceptable, or are they manipulation of a disaster for financial gain?*

🖾 *In 1979 Lord Grade produced his film, 'Raise the Titanic', rumoured to cost more than the ship itself. Lord Grade remarked to his shareholders: "'Raise the Titanic'? It would have been cheaper to lower the Atlantic!*

♪ Abide with me; Eternal Father, strong to save (for those in peril on the sea)

1 On this day in 1989, 96 Liverpool United football fans were crushed to death in Sheffield's Hillsborough Stadium. We're going to listen to a poem about the events of that day:

2 To Sheffield we went, expectant and proud
With faces aglow, singing aloud,
Grandads and kids and ordinary blokes
Full of patter and Merseyside jokes,
That hide the pain of struggling for bread
To follow the feats of our boys in red.

3 Through turnstyles, gates and tunnel
The excited crowd began to funnel.
Though pressure grew, good nature prevailed
But some felt faint and others paled,
The small and weak were spared some pain
By strong protectors who took up the strain.

4 As the Reds appeared we swelled our song
Which carried outside to the waiting throng,
Whose frustration burst as the whistle blew
To start the match they'd paid to see, too,
As life started oozing from being pressed,
Gates were flung open to ease their distress.

5 The dam was breached, the flood swept in,
Increasing the pressure on those within,
Trapped like animals in an iron cage
Solidly built to contain the rage
Of hooligan, punk, thug and brute
Who have brought our nation into disrepute.

6 Distress changed to panic and then despair
As loved ones crushed, gasped for air
Spring-sweet, abundant just inches away
But denied by a cage on that terrible day.
We'd gone to count goals by our boys in red
But shed bitter tears as we counted our dead.

7 Now a city in shock
mourns those who have died
And nobody knows who should be tried
For the carnage, pain, grief and sorrows
That must be faced through endless tomorrows,
But of this I am certain, history will say
There were more saints than sinners
on that dreadful day.

8 Let's pause in silence for a moment for all who suffer tragedies in their lives…

(pause)

📖 Could use the prayer from 8 April.

📖 The author of the poem has not been traced.

📖 "bread" – money

📖 "the Reds" – Liverpool United;

📖 "denied by a cage" – security fencing around the perimeter of the pitch.

📖 In the mid-1980s in Britain it became a custom, here and there, to leave some flowers at the place where someone had died tragically. More than a million people visited Liverpool's ground of Anfield in the days after the Hillsborough disaster, leaving flowers on the pitch. It is only since Hillsborough in 1989 that the practice of leaving flowers at the site of sudden death has become more widespread, and we now see bunches of flowers tied to lampposts to commemorate the death of someone in a traffic accident, and flowers are often renewed in those places at the anniversary of death. Most memorably, at the funeral of Diana, Princess of Wales, in September 1997, many thousands of bouquets of flowers were laid in public places and thrown onto the road along which her coffin was being driven.

🎼 Abide with me; The Lord's my shepherd

16 APRIL

1 In Korea there is a story told, a legend,
about a man who dies
and goes to Heaven.
Before he enters Heaven
he says to the gatekeeper,
"Before I go into Heaven
I'd like you to take me
on a tour of Hell."

2 And so the man is taken, first of all,
to visit Hell.
When he gets there
he is surprised to see a long table
piled high with the finest food
anyone could ever want.
But he saw that the people in Hell
were starving,
and he asked his guide:
"Why is everyone starving?"

3 "It's like this," said the guide.
"Everybody who comes to Hell
is given a pair of chopsticks
- two metres long,
and they have to hold them at the end
at mealtimes.
Of course, no-one can eat
with chopsticks that long.
Look at everyone
lifting their chopsticks,
trying to feed themselves
- they miss their mouths every time.
How miserable they all look!"

4 The man agreed
that this really was Hell,
and he asked
to be taken straight back to Heaven.
When he arrived in Heaven
he saw the same kind of table
piled high with the very same food.
But here the people looked so very happy.

5 "No chopsticks, I suppose?"
asked the man.
"Oh yes," said his guide.

"They have the same chopsticks,
two metres long,
and they must be held at the end:
the same as in Hell.
But, here in Heaven,
these people have learned
that as they feed their neighbour
with the long chopsticks,
their neighbour feeds them."

6 *Let us pray:*

**Lord, inspire me always
to have genuine care and concern
    for others,
and may people be as generous to me
as I am to them.
Amen.**

 If I am lacking love; O Lord all the world
belongs to you

1   Benjamin Franklin was an American diplomat, but also a scientist, becoming the inventor of the lightning conductor. After the War of Independence between Britain and the American colonies, Franklin was one of those who wrote the Constitution for the newly independent United States of America. He died on this day in 1790.

2   One day, Benjamin Franklin gave someone a list of practical suggestions about getting along with others. This is what he wrote:

3   *"The best thing to give your enemy is forgiveness;*
    - to an opponent, tolerance;
    - to a friend, your ear;

4   *- to your child, good example;*
    - to your father, reverence;
    - to your mother, conduct that will make her proud of you;
    - to yourself, respect;
    - to all people, love."

5   *Let us pray:*

Lord, give me patience and tolerance with everyone.
Lord, show me
how to be kind and generous
to everyone.
Lord, help me
to live positively and cheerfully
for everyone.
Amen.

✍ *Prior to reading Ben Franklin's quote, students could be invited to make a list of what they think might be the best thing to give to others, listing: "an opponent, a friend, your child, your father, your mother, yourself, all people." Others could be added e.g. sister/brother, someone on your sports team, sports manager, boss at work, prime minister.*

🎼 If I am lacking love; O Lord all the world belongs to you

18 APRIL

(See also 14 March & 18 May)

1   Albert Einstein was born in Germany in 1879. He is now acknowledged as one of the world's greatest scientists. Yet, when he applied to attend a college in Munich, he was turned down because they said that he "showed no promise". He worked in different jobs to get the money he needed to follow his scientific interests.

2   Important as knowledge is, without his sense of imagination and creativity he would not have been able to make use of his knowledge to make such advances in science. It's interesting that he said:

   "Imagination is more important than knowledge."

3   Einstein also said:

   "When I see the Cosmos, I can't help but believe that there is a Divine Hand behind it all."

4   He died on this day in 1955, having said that

   "Only a life lived for others is worthwhile."

5   *Let us pray:*

   **Lord our God,
   you give different gifts to each of us
   and you are pleased
   when we use our gifts well.
   Inspire each of us to reach our potential
   and use our gifts
   for the benefit of others.
   Enable us by the power of your Spirit
   to grow in faith
   and in imagination and creativity,
   living a life for others
   that is worthwhile.
   Amen.**

✍ *Scientific advances have been made possible because of Einstein's contributions regarding the quantum theory of light; his knowledge of molecular motion; and his Theory of Relativity which centres around his equation that $E = mc^2$ where E = energy, m = mass of the particle, and c = velocity of light*

1 The three main religions in the world - Judaism, Christianity, and Islam - all believe in one God. Jews sometimes call him "Yahweh", and Muslims call him "Allah".

2 Muslims follow the religion of Islam, and their holy book is called the Qur'an (Koran). Muslims believe that it is the message of God spoken by the Angel Gabriel to Mohammed, who died in the year 632 AD. The Qu'ran is written in Arabic.

3 From an early age, Muslims read from the Qur'an each day. Their holy book is so important to them that they learn parts of it by heart, and many learn the whole of the Qur'an by heart. The prayer we are going to use is based on the opening lines of the Qur'an. Members of each of the three world religions could use this prayer together:

4 *Let us pray:*

In the name of God, who is merciful:
All praise be to God,
who is the Lord of everything.
We serve no-one but you, our God,
and you are the only one
to whom we turn for help.
Keep us away from the path
of those who stray from you.
Guide us instead
on the way we should go
- on the path
of those whom you have blessed.

📖 *The Qur'an [Koran] is the holy book of Islam. The word "Qur'an" means "recitation".*

📖 *The Christian's Bible is in two parts. The New Testament [a word that means Agreement or Relationship] starts with the Gospels of Jesus; the Old Testament is everything before Jesus. What Christians call the "Old Testament" is the Scriptures of the Jews. All three religions - Judaism, Christianity, and Islam, believe in only one God - they are called the monotheistic religions - and they all look to Abraham [whom we read about in Genesis 12-25] as their "father in faith".*

 Oh the love of my Lord is the essence

20 APRIL

1 Tomorrow, 21st April, is one of the days when the British National Anthem is played the most. Some radio stations, for example, will play it early in the day. 21st April is the birthday of Queen Elizabeth II.

2 The tune of what we now know as "God save our Gracious Queen" (or King) is based on a piece written in 1619 by an English composer.

3 Britain had governed what is now the United States of America until the Declaration of Independence in 1776. The tune of the old British anthem was kept, but was used with new words - either "God save George Washington" or "God save the Thirteen States" (being the number of States in the USA at the time of Independence). The United States' present anthem ("The Star-Spangled Banner") officially became their national anthem only in 1931 - both tunes were in use until then.

4 The tune of "God save our Gracious Queen" has also been used in the past as the national anthems of Denmark, Russia, Sweden, Switzerland, and in parts of what is now Germany. The small country of Liechtenstein is the only country still to use for its national anthem the same tune as the British national anthem.

5 Let's pray the shortest psalm in the Bible. It invites people - not of any **single** country but the people of **all** nations - to give praise to God:

6 *Let us pray:*

Praise the Lord, all you nations.
Speak to him, all people of the earth,
  because his love is great
  and he is always faithful.

(Psalm 117)

📖 *The anthem's tune was composed in 1619 by Dr John Bull.*

📖 *Queen Elizabeth II was born 21/4/1926. She also has an "Official Birthday" - the second Saturday in the month of June - when State ceremonies can be held in London.*

🎶 Christ is our king, let the whole world rejoice

APRIL 21

1 The author, Mark Twain, died on this day in 1901. He wrote *'The Prince and the Pauper'*. His two most famous books - *'Tom Sawyer'* and *'Huckleberry Finn'* are set in the southern United States where he was born. His name at birth was Samuel Clemens, but he wanted to choose a different name (a "pen name") under which to write.

2 Samuel Clemens had worked as a river pilot with boatmen along the great River Mississippi, over 2,300 miles *(3,700 kilometres)* in length. A century ago, when boat captains wanted to know if the water below them was shallow, a sailor would let into the water a length of weighted twain (string), already measured out at two fathoms (12 feet or 3.6 metres). "Mark twain" would be the shout of the sailor when the boat was in shallow water, and so the captain would know to be very careful. Hearing those two words so often, Samuel Clemens decided to adopt them as his pen-name under which to write his books.

3 Mark Twain made many interesting comments throughout his life. On one occasion he said: *"I can live for six months on a compliment."*

4 Let's each think in silence for a moment of **two** occasions when good things were said of us, and how we felt on receiving those compliments.

(pause...)

5 Let's each think in silence for a moment of **two** people we can encourage today with a genuine compliment - one person at home, and one person in school or at work. Let's think what we might say to them when the time is right...

(pause...)

6 *Let us pray:*

**Father, that I may treat others
  as I would like them to treat me.
That I may forgive others
  as I would like them to forgive me.
That I may encourage
  and compliment others
  in the same way
  that I would like them
  to encourage me.
That I may see and love in others
  what I would like them
  to see and love in me.
These things I ask
  through Christ our Lord.
Amen.**

🖂 *Samuel Langhorne Clemens (Mark Twain): 30/11/1835-21/4/ 1910*

🖂 *Other terms for "pen name" are "nom de plume" and "pseudonym"*

♪ Do not be afraid; I heard the Lord call my name

22 APRIL

1 Let's remind ourselves in silence that we are in God's presence…

   (pause…)

2 The word "prophet" means "God's spokesman". It's **not** anything to do with trying to discover what's going to happen in the future.

3 We read of the prophets (God's spokesmen) in the Old Testament. One of the prophets was called Micah. He spoke very simply about three qualities that are needed to live a good life:

4 *"To act justly,*
   to love tenderly,
   and to walk humbly with God

   (Micah 6^8)

5 *We make that our prayer today:*

   That we may act justly,
   love tenderly,
   and walk humbly with you, our God.

6 They are easy words to remember, and they are the kind of words that some people learn and repeat a few times during the day, reminding themselves that God is with them.

📖 *The "Old Testament" is everything in the Bible before Jesus.*

 This is what Yahweh asks of you; Come let us go up to the Lord; I give my hands

1 Today is Saint George's Day, the patron saint of England, and we pray for all English people.

2 It is also the day on which William Shakespeare was born in 1564. He died on his birthday in 1616.

3 In his play, Richard II, *(the second)* Shakespeare has one of his characters say:

"I count myself
in nothing else so happy
as in a soul
remembering my good friends."
                    (Richard II,Act 2, Scene 3)

4 Each of us can think for a moment of a few individuals who have improved the quality of our lives, whom we remember as good friends.

(pause...)

5 In Shakespeare's play, King Henry VI, *(the sixth)* the king says:

"O Lord, that lends me life,
Lend me a heart replete with thankfulness."
('King Henry the Sixth', Part 2, Act 1,Scene 1)

6 *Let's take these ideas and pray:*

Lord, as you lend me life,
  lend me a heart full of thankfulness,
  that I may treasure good friends
  and be appreciative
  of all who are part of my life.
Inspire me each day
  to live positively and cheerfully,
  living in such a way
  that I express thanks
    and encouragement
  to others,
  so that, together,
  we may bring out the best
    in each other.
Amen.

✍ *"replete" = full*

✍ *In the first passage - from 'Richard II' - it is Bolingbroke, the future King Henry IV, (the fourth) who says these words about good friends.*

✍ *Jesus said: "I shall not call you servants any more; I call you friends." - John 15[14-15]*

✍ *Also in Shakespeare, "This royal throne of kings, this sceptred isle." is to be found in 'Richard II' , Act 2, Scene 1.*

✍ *Spoken by Polonius in 'Hamlet', Act 1,Scene 3:*
"To thine own self be true,
And it must follow, as the night the day,
Thou canst not then be false to any man."

🎵 Thank you for fathers; Father I place into your hands; Thank you for giving me the morning; Happy the man *[which incorporates part of the Hamlet quote]*

24 APRIL

1 Beside the River Thames in London are the buildings called the Houses of Parliament or the Palace of Westminster. The previous buildings had been destroyed by fire in 1834.

2 The tall clock tower is often called "Big Ben", even though the name actually is only that of the great bell that strikes, weighing nearly 14 tonnes. "Big Ben", the bell, was hung in the tower on this day in 1858. It strikes the musical note 'E', and is the most broadcast bell in the world. We can hear it at the start of 'News at Ten', and it is sometimes broadcast on the radio, here and to countries overseas. During the Second World War, when most of Europe was occupied by the Nazis, the broadcast of the ringing of the bell helped give people hope of freedom.

3 And so, when people across the world hear the ringing of 'Big Ben', or see pictures of the tower, they see it as a sign or symbol of many things - hope, freedom, what it means to be a Londoner or English or British, our political system of democracy with a parliament. Seeing or hearing "Big Ben" gives various messages to people.

4 I can ask what people might "see" and "hear" when they meet me. What are the "messages" that people pick up from me? What do people learn about me from the way I live, from the way I do things, and from my attitude?

5 Let's pause in silence for a moment, for each of us to think of the character-impression we make on others - what people might "see" and "hear" when they are with us...

(pause...)

6 *Let us pray:*

Loving Lord,
we need the power of your Spirit
in our lives
to build on what is good,
and to help change
what needs to be changed.
We pray that we may be faithful
in responding to your call to grow
as the people you have called us to be,
that we may ring out your praises
through the way we live each day.
Amen.

🔊 *The 7 metre [23 foot] diameter clock faces were seen in the film 'The 39 Steps', as Robert Powell hung to one of the hands of the clock. "Big Ben" is probably named after Sir Benjamin Hall, a big and heavy man who was Parliament's Commissioner of Works.*
"St Stephen's Tower" - which we often call "Big Ben" - is the name of the tower in which the bell hangs.

🔊 *The four bells of Liverpool's RC Cathedral are called Matthew, Mark, Luke and John, as a reminder that we, too, are called to live and "ring out"/broadcast the Good News of the Gospel.*

🔊 *"If I speak without love, I am simply a gong booming" - 1 Cor 13[1]*

🎵 God's Spirit is in my heart; Christ is our king, let the whole world rejoice; Colours of day; Follow me; Give me joy in my heart; If I am lacking love; I watch the sunrise

1 A Russian called Anthony Bloom was an atheist when he was a university student in Paris. Simply to please somebody, he attended a meeting to which a Russian priest had been invited. Anthony Bloom hated the thought of being there, and grew more and more annoyed at what he heard about Christ and Christianity. When he got back home he asked his mother for a copy of the Gospels, because he wanted to prove that the priest had been lying.

2 Anthony decided to read quickly one of the Gospels. He counted the number of chapters in each of the four Gospels, and found that the Gospel of Saint Mark was the shortest - he didn't want to waste too much time reading what he thought was rubbish!

3 Before he reached the third chapter of Saint Mark's Gospel, he became aware of a Presence on the other side of the table. He became so sure that the Presence was the Risen Jesus, that his life changed forever. He became a Christian, and later became a priest. He is now an archbishop in the Russian Orthodox Church.

4 From having hated all that he thought Christianity was about, Anthony Bloom's life changed when he had some kind of experience that Jesus was alive and was beside him. It was St Mark's Gospel that he had read, and today is the feastday of Saint Mark.

5 *Let us pray:*

Lord Jesus,
 we remember that you said
 that you would be with us,
 so we do know in our minds
 that you are present.
But there's a difference

between knowing that you're present
and growing in the faith
that you are beside us.
We ask for the power of your Spirit
in our lives each day,
so that we may live more fully
in your presence.
Only then will our attitude
and words and actions
better reflect yours. Amen.

🖎 *"atheist" - someone who does not believe that God exists.*

🖎 *Fuller details of Anthony Bloom's experiences can be found in his book, 'School for Prayer' - DLT, 1970*

🖎 *Luke 24$^{13-35}$ - 2 disciples walking to Emmaus, not recognising the Risen Jesus walking with them.*

🖎 *Of the four gospels that we have, St Mark's was the first to be written - about 65 AD, from Rome. Much of his information and details were given to him by eye-witness Simon Peter. Mark wrote for Christians of non-Jewish background.*

🖎 *for details of Mark [sometimes called "John Mark"], look at Acts 12^{12,25}, Acts 15^5; Col 4^{10}; 2 Tim 4^{11}; 1 Peter 5^{13}; and probably Mark 14^{51}.*
St Mark is the Patron of Venice.

🎼 Christ be beside me; Yahweh, I know you are near; In you, my God; Walk with me, O my Lord

26 APRIL

1 It was on this day in 1986 that the whole world learned the name of a small town, 80 miles *(130 km)* north of Kiev in The Ukraine. The town was Chernobyl, and The Ukraine is now an independent country but, at that time, was part of the Soviet Union, before the Fall of Communism.

2 12 miles *(20 km)* outside the town of Chernobyl is a nuclear power plant. Some of the people operating the nuclear power plant wanted to conduct an experiment with the water-cooling system. To do this, they decided to switch off the safety systems, which were designed to cut off the nuclear reaction if there were any problems.

3 One of the nuclear reactors went out of control. If the engineers had not overridden the safety systems, the reactors would have switched themselves off when they became dangerous. The engineers made a wrong decision, with disastrous consequences, and a steam explosion caused the reactor's protective covering and roof to be blown off - the roof weighed hundreds of tonnes. Vast amounts of radiation were released.

4 Far too late, 100,000 people were evacuated from towns miles around. By that time, radiation was being carried by high air currents across Europe. Detectors in Sweden were the first to alert the rest of Europe as to what was happening. Those detectors showed that the radiation in Sweden - 800 miles *(1300km)* away from Chernobyl - was high. The fallout of radiation in Britain was such as to cause concern in agriculture, and for some months it was forbidden to eat Welsh lamb - lambs that had eaten the grass that had been exposed to the radiation that had spread from 1500 miles away.

5 The greatest concern, of course, was for the many people far more seriously affected by the radiation - they were within a hundred miles of Chernobyl. Over the following months, many of the children developed leukemia and other forms of cancer, and some of the sick children were invited to Britain and other countries for holidays.

6 That decision to cut off the safety system cost the lives of many people. That irresponsible choice left vast areas of their country so radiated that no-one will be able to live there again.

7 *Let us pray:*

God our Father,
  with the gifts you have given to us
  we have responsibilities and duties.
Lead us to do our best
  and act responsibly.
Give us courage
  when we face difficulties.
Inspire us to make our choices wisely,
  always remembering
  that there are consequences
  to what we choose to do.
Amen.

1 Yesterday, 26th April, in 1994, saw the start of voting in South Africa's first elections to include people of all colours. "The Rainbow Nation" is the phrase often used by President Nelson Mandela about South Africa's multi-racial society.

2 We are going to listen to a translation of some of the words of South Africa's new National Anthem. We can make the words our own prayer for our own nation:

3 *Let us pray:*

**Bless our nation, Lord,
  and let your mercy come among us.
Let justice triumph in our land
  as we live and strive for freedom.
Let our people stand before you
  as you come to judge us.
Stretch out your hands, O Lord,
  and have compassion on us.**

📖 *The new National Anthem is called "Nkosi Sikileli Afrika".*

📖 *"Apartheid" had been the political system in South Africa from 1948 until 1990. "Apartheid" means "separateness", and people had been kept apart and discriminated against according to the colour of their skin.*

📖 *See also 10 May; 12,18 July*

🎵 Come, let us go up to the mountain of the Lord; Christ is our king

28 APRIL

1 A group of medical students were discussing the various tests that can be made on the foetus in the womb to discover if there are handicaps. The lecturer said to all the students:

"About the termination of a pregnancy, I would like your opinion. The father had syphilis; the mother had tuberculosis. Of the four children born, the first was blind, the second died, the third was deaf and dumb, the fourth child had tuberculosis. The mother is pregnant with a fifth child. Given the conditions of the other children, should the mother terminate that pregnancy?" A vote was taken, and an overwhelming number said that she should have an abortion.

2 The lecturer replied: *"If abortion had been available in those days, and your advice was taken, you would have aborted the great composer, Beethoven."*

3 Yesterday - 27 April, 1967, Britain's Abortion Act was passed by Parliament.

4 *Let us pray:*

God our Father,
  inspire us with a great respect
  for all human life
  from the time of the child
  growing in the womb
  to the point of death.
May that respect lead us
  to grow in a sense of responsibility
  for all our brothers and sisters
  throughout the world,
  knowing that,
    where one person suffers
  and is degraded,
  all of humanity
    is belittled and abused.
May we grow in a sense of love and care
  for those less fortunate
    than ourselves,

and lead us to do something
about the difficulites in our world.
Amen.

🕮 *"Termination of a pregnancy"* is another term for abortion. In 1996 there were 177,225 abortions in England and Wales.

🕮 In 1997 social workers in India discovered that for every aborted male there were 1000 aborted females

🕮 Isaiah 49$^{15-16}$ - "could a woman ever forget her baby?"

🕮 The Abortion Act came into effect on 23 October 1967. See also 23 October.

🎵 I will never forget you, my people; Oh the word of my Lord; Do not be afraid

1   April 29th 1933 saw the first football match in which players wore numbered shirts. Everton wore numbers 1 (the goalie) to 11, and Manchester City wore the numbers 12 to 22 (their goalie).

2   As we know, the shirts of most professionals now bear their name as well as their number.

3   Calling people by their names is considered to be a sign of respect and of wanting to relate to them. In some countries, prisoners are never called by their names, but always by a number. When asked who they are, the prisoners must state only their number. It is a way of "de-humanising" people, and taking their "individuality" away from them.

4   *Let us pray:*

Lord Jesus,
  when you met Zacchaeus,
  the tax collector
  whom everyone hated,
  you looked at him
  and called him by his name.
In doing that,
  you gave him back his dignity,
  and he changed his life around.
He was able to see himself
  in a better way,
  and so he gave back to others
  the money he had cheated
    from them.
Lead us to show respect
  for each person as an individual,
  treating others in the same way
  that we would like to be treated.
Amen.

🖅 *Everton won the 1933 Cup Final 3-0*

🖅 *Zacchaeus - Luke 19$^{1-10}$*

🖅 *See also ideas and the prayer for 23 January.*

🎼 Do not be afraid; O Lord all the world belongs to you

1 A German-speaking boy was often physically abused - beaten by his father for the smallest thing he ever did wrong. The father did not call him by his name. Instead, whenever the father wanted the boy to come to him, he whistled for him, as if his son was a dog.

2 Sometime later, the boy discovered that his grandfather (whom he hardly knew) was Jewish. In his twisted way of thinking, he thought that his grandfather's "Jewishness" somehow must be the reason why his father was so cruel and nasty towards him.

3 Having been insulted and abused by his father, the boy grew up with strange views about himself, and with strange views about Jewish people. This boy was Adolf Hitler.

4 After leading Germany and Europe and much of the world in devastation and war, costing the lives of so many people (including millions of Jews), Adolf Hitler committed suicide on this day in 1945 in his bunker deep under the ruined city of Berlin.

5 *Let us pray in silence for a moment, thinking of all who died during that war...*

   (pause...)

6 Let us pray for all who suffer
   from hatred and prejudice,
   from abuse and ill-treatment,
   and for all who are victims
   of other people.
Let us pray, too,
   for the people of violence,
   that they may change their ways
   and learn to respect others.
Let us pray for ourselves,
   that when we face
   what is negative or evil
we may have
the courage and generosity
to break the cycle of violence,
taking responsibility
for the direction
in which we want our lives to go.
Let us pray
   that we may always do to others
   as we would wish them to do to us.
Amen.

❖❖❖❖❖❖❖❖❖❖❖❖❖❖❖❖❖

 *Adolf Hitler was born in German-speaking Austria.*

142

Moveable
Feasts

FAMILY FAST DAY

(See also Family Fast Day in Volume 3)

1 Saint Ambrose was born about the year 339. He wrote:

*"It is not from your own possessions
that you are bestowing gifts on the poor;
you are but restoring to them
what is theirs by right
- for what was given to everyone
for the use of all
you have taken for **your** exclusive use.
The earth belongs - not to the rich
- but to everyone.
So, far from giving lavishly,
you are only paying part of your debt."*

2 Another Christian - Saint Basil - living at the same time, said:

*"The food you have stored away
belongs to the hungry.
The unworn garment in your wardrobe
belongs to the naked.
The gold you have hidden away
belongs to the poor."*

3. *Let us pray:*

**On this day, Lord,
when we particularly think of others,
lead us to live fully
our common humanity -
respecting others
and sharing with them
what they need.
Show us how to get our priorities right
and live simply,
so that others may simply live.
Amen.**

📖 *St Ambrose died in Milan on 4th April 397.*

📖 *St Basil died on 1st January 379 in Caesarea in Cappadocia in what is now Turkey.*

📖 *Matthew 25[31-46]: hungry, thirsty, stranger, naked, sick, in prison.*

📖 *Luke 16[19-31]: The rich man and the poor man called Lazarus [NB: not the same Lazarus as was raised from the dead]*

📖 *CAFOD, Romero Close, Stockwell Road, London SW9 9TY Tel: 0171-733-7900*

📖 *See also 16 March*

🎵 Follow me; O Lord, all the world; This is what Yahweh asks of you.

THE DAYS OF LENT

Lent starts on Ash Wednesday. If we count the days before the Resurrection on Easter Sunday, they total 46, not 40! The Sundays are not counted in the "40 days of Lent" because **every** Sunday recalls the Resurrection. Lent is 40 *weekdays* before Easter Sunday.

The number 40 has a special significance in the Bible. It is written that the Great Flood lasted for 40 days and nights when Noah was saved *(Gen 7)*. When the Israelites left slavery in Egypt, they wandered for 40 years in the desert before reaching the Promised Land *(Ex 16^{35})*. During that time, Moses spent 40 days on Mt Sinai, meeting God and receiving the 10 Commandments *(Ex 24^{18})*. The length of rule of various leaders and kings was 40 years e.g. King David *(1 Chr 29^{27})* and King Solomon *(2 Chr 9^{30})*. The prophet Elijah fasted for 40 days *(1 Kings 19$^{1-8}$)*. The prophet

Jonah was told that in 40 days Nineveh would be destroyed *(Jonah 3^4)*. Jesus fasted for 40 days *(Mt 4^2)*, and for 40 days after his death and resurrection, Jesus appeared until he ascended to the Father *(Acts 1^3)*.

Holy Week is the name given to the week that starts with Palm Sunday and finishes with Holy Saturday.

✍ *Lent in the Eastern Churches is **fifty** weekdays because they count both days of the weekend - Saturday and Sunday - as family celebration times.*

✍ *It was during the season of Lent that Anthony Bloom unexpectedly felt the Presence of Christ. See the account as given for 25 April.*

THE DAYS OF LENT

SUNDAY	MONDAY	TUESDAY	WEDNESDAY	THURSDAY	FRIDAY	SATURDAY
		(Shrove Tuesday)	Ash Wednesday			
1st Sunday of Lent						
2nd Sunday of Lent						
3rd Sunday of Lent						
4th Sunday of Lent						
5th Sunday of Lent						
Palm/Passion Sunday				Holy Thursday	Good Friday	Holy Saturday
EASTER SUNDAY						

SHROVE TUESDAY

1 Tomorrow, Ash Wednesday, sees the start of Lent, which is a period of 40 days' preparation for the great feast of Easter,when Jesus rose from the dead. Lent is also a time for looking again at our priorities, and turning away from sinfulness.

2 Lent's 40 days call to mind particularly that Jesus fasted for 40 days in the desert.

3 In the Old Testament we can think of the 40 years that the Israelites spent in the desert before they reached the Promised Land. During that time, Moses spent 40 days on Mount Sinai where he met God and received the 10 Commandments. Elijah, one of the great prophets, spent 40 days fasting

4 "Shrove Tuesday" is the name sometimes given to today, the day before Lent starts. "Shrove" is a word meaning "confessing our sins", and this used to be the day when people would confess their sins to a priest before Lent started. Nowadays many people receive the Sacrament of Reconciliation - sometimes still called "Confession" - during Lent itself.

5 As the 40 days of Lent were a serious time of fasting, Shrove Tuesday would be the last day for eating in the usual way.

6 Food that was in the house would be used up on this day - especially the kinds of food that people were forbidden to eat during Lent - and so any fat, eggs and flour were used up by mixing them together to make pancakes. Sometimes we simply call the day "Pancake Tuesday".

7 In other parts of the world, Carnivals are held in the days before Lent starts. The word "Carnival" means "finishing with meat" as, years ago, no meat would be eaten during Lent itself.

8 One of the most colourful of carnivals is "Mardi Gras", which can last a few days, finishing on this day. The words "Mardi Gras" are French for "Fat Tuesday", again reminding us of the last opportunity for a great feast before the start of Lent! This festival has dancing in the streets, floats, costumes, music, processions, and acting. The most famous Mardi Gras carnivals are held in Rio de Janeiro in Brazil, and New Orleans in the southern United States.

9 *Let us pray:*

Father,
   we read at the beginning of the Bible
   that you see all that you have made
   and you proclaim it to be good.
Your Son, Jesus, was life-affirming
   in all that he said and did,
   rejoicing in the lilies of the field
   and the birds of the air.
He lived fully his human life,
   and the first sign that he gave
   that your Kingdom was amongst us
   was to turn water into wine
   at the marriage-feast of Cana
   - and we are told
   that the wine he made
   for the celebration
   was the very best!

10 We read in the gospel
   that Jesus was criticised
   for eating and celebrating with sinners.
He told the story of the Prodigal Son,
   and we hear
   that the father rejoiced
   and put on a feast
   when his lost son returned to him.
In the same way, Father,
   you look out for us
   and rejoice and celebrate
   when we return
   to the fullness of life
   that Jesus offered.

It is in and through
  our common humanity
  - which Jesus himself shared -
  that we are called
  to wholeness and holiness.
Show us, Father, how to be fully alive,
  rejoicing with those who rejoice
  and bringing comfort
  to those who are in sorrow.
Amen.

📣 *An Old English word "scrifen" has given us "shriven" and "shrove", meaning "to confess one's sins". The Sunday, Monday and Tuesday directly before Ash Wednesday were once called "Shrovetide", as people confessed their sins prior to the start of Lent. Nowadays Lent itself is the time for repentance prior to the celebration of the Resurrection at Easter.*

📣 *The word "carnival" comes from Latin: "carnis" - flesh/meat, and "levare" - to put away.*

📣 *Other famous Mardi Gras carnivals are held in Nice in southern France, and Cologne in Germany.*

📣 *Biblical references in the prayer [in paragraph order] are:*
Gen 1^{31}, Lk 12^{22-32}, Jn 2^{1-12}, Lk 5^{30}, Lk 15^{11-32}, Jn 10^{10}, Rom 12^{15}.)

📣 *The words "whole" and "holy" both come from the same stem: "hal" in Old English.*

📣 *T.S.Eliot in "Little Gidding" says that holiness is "a condition of complete simplicity costing not less than everything."*

🎼 Come back to me; God forgave my sin; Look around you, can you see; Rejoice in the Lord always; Rejoice, rejoice, Christ is in you

147

ASH WEDNESDAY

1 **Why are we gathered here?**

2 We have gathered together to mark the beginning of Lent.

3 **How long is Lent?**

4 Lent is 40 weekdays, calling to mind that Jesus fasted and prayed for 40 days before he began to spread the gospel.

5 **Why is this day called "Ash Wednesday"?**

6 We have burnt the palm leaves used on last year's Palm Sunday, giving us ashes. Ashes remind us of the deadly things in our lives - when we choose death and not life by being selfish. Ashes remind us that we need to die to selfishness so as to mature and grow in Christ.

7 **Why do we put ashes on our heads?**

8 It's a sign that's been used for over two thousand years - a sign that we want to make some changes in our lives. We want to "turn over a new leaf", leave the past behind us and make a new start.

9 **What are we asked to do in Lent?**

10 Lent is a time for sorting out our priorities. Lent offers the opportunity to make a new start and believe in God's love for us. When ashes are given, we sometimes hear these words: *"Turn away from sin, and believe in the Gospel."* We think of the choices we make, and we believe more fully in God's love for us.

11 *Let us pray:*

Lord Jesus,
   as Lent begins
   we ask for the power of your Spirit
   that we may become
   more thoughtful towards others,
   more honest with ourselves,
   and more faithful to you.
Help us to walk in your presence
   and grow as the people
   you want us to be.   Amen.

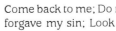 Come back to me; Do not be afraid; God forgave my sin; Look around you, can you see? Oh the word of my Lord

148

PALM/PASSION SUNDAY

1 Jesus made his way to the capital city, Jerusalem, realising what the consequences would be of all that he had said and done. He would be rejected and, in a few days' time, would be tortured and killed.

2 On Palm Sunday, Jesus arrived in Jerusalem and many people greeted him, thinking that he was a new king coming to power, who would somehow drive out the Roman occupation soldiers. Jesus rode on a donkey instead of on a warrior's horse. Great crowds of people spread their cloaks on the road, and others cut down palm branches to wave to greet him. They quoted well-known words from one of the psalms:

3 *"Blessed is he*
who comes in the name of the Lord.
Hosanna in the highest."

4 Yet, in a few days' time, some of those now cheering him on this journey, would mock him on his final journey to the cross.

5 *Let us pray:*

Lord Jesus,
open our eyes to recognise you
as you walk beside us,
accompanying us
on our journey in life each day.
Give us the same courage and
determination
that you needed
as you faced your future
and the people of Jerusalem.
Amen.

🔊 *"Holy Week" is the name given to the week that starts with Palm Sunday and finishes with Holy Saturday.*

🔊 *The "hosanna" quote is from Psalm 118$^{22\text{-}23}$ Nowadays we use the same words during Mass before starting the Eucharist Prayer.*

🔊 *Mk 11$^{1\text{-}11}$; Mt 21$^{1\text{-}11}$; Lk 19$^{28\text{-}38}$; Jn 12$^{12\text{-}19}$*

🎼 From heaven you came (the Servant King); Give me joy in my heart; My song is love unknown

HOLY THURSDAY

1 One of Leonardo da Vinci's finest paintings is "The Last Supper", showing Jesus and his 12 apostles sitting at the table. The large fresco is painted on a dining room wall in a monastery in Milan, northern Italy, and shows the moment when Jesus says: "One of you will betray me."

2 As Leonardo thought of how he would give different faces and expressions to each of the 13 figures, a particular person came to mind - someone who was jealous of him, who caused him a lot of trouble, and influenced others to think less of Leonardo. The idea came to the artist that he could use this painting to get back at his enemy by painting the face of that man as Judas, who betrayed Jesus. Leonardo told a few friends what he intended to do, and they all laughed.

3 It took Leonardo over two years to finish the great painting, and many gathered in the room for Leonardo to unveil it. As he removed the curtain, everyone saw the beauty of the painting and also that Leonardo had, indeed, included the face of his enemy - but not as Judas. Instead, he had painted his enemy's face as that of Jesus.

4 Leonardo's action had changed an enemy into a friend.

5. Let us pray:

Father, there are people
who have done wrong to me,
just as I have done wrong to others.
On this special day, Father,
forgive me the wrong I have done,
in the same way
as I set out to forgive others
and hold no grudges against them.
Inspire me to break the cycle
of hatred and evil

whenever I come across them,
and lead me always
to grow in your love. Amen.

A variation on this story [and only one account can be accurate] has Leonardo with only one more apostle to paint - Judas, the traitor. He walks through the streets and eventually finds a down-and-out man who looks hardened and treacherous. They return and, as Leonardo starts to copy the man's face as that of Judas, he tells the man that he looks a little familiar, and asks him if they have ever met. "Yes," says the man, "but a lot has changed in my life since you first painted me a couple of years ago. You picked me out from the choir in which I sang, and you copied my face as the portrait of Jesus."

The fresco is painted on the refectory wall of the Monastery of Santa Maria delle Grazia in Milan. Leonardo used an experimental technique of painting with oil on dry plaster. Sadly, deterioration set in only three or four years after its completion. Restoration was attempted over the years, culminating with use of the latest technology in 1977.

Leonardo was born in the small town of Vinci, near Florence in northern Italy, on 15/4/1452. He died on 2/5/1519.

We remember that, on this day, Jesus said: "A new commandment I give you: love one another. When people see this love you have for one another, they will know that you are my disciples" [John 13[34]].
"Commandment" - or "rule" - in Latin is "mandatum", giving us the former name for this day: "Maundy Thursday", calling to mind the new commandment that Jesus gave us, "to love one another". From the same source we get our word "mandatory", when we say, for example, that a speed limit is "mandatory" - obligatory, the rule. A "mandate" is an official order e.g. the United Nations mandating one country to govern some land. A government may talk of a "mandate" being given by the people in an election.

📖 *From the year 600 until 1689, when William III and Mary II came to the British throne as joint rulers, kings and queens washed the feet of some poor people each Maundy Thursday. This tradition called to mind that Jesus had washed the feet of his disciples on that day, symbolising his love for them [John 13$^{1-20}$]. Since 1689 the king or queen has given clothes or money instead. Now it is always money that is given. The ceremony takes place in a different cathedral each year, with the "Maundy Money" being given to local people who have been chosen because of lengthy service given to their local church or community. One man and one woman are chosen for each year that the king or queen has lived. The "Maundy Money" is a set of specially-minted penny coins: the same number again as the age of the monarch. The coins, of course, are worth far more than their face value. For example, on Maundy Thursday 1997, the 71-year old Queen Elizabeth II gave 71 penny coins to 71 men and 71 women in Bradford Cathedral.*

📖 *Poem: "Love bade me welcome" by George Herbert*

📖 *See also the Supplement at the back of Volume 2 for the Feast of 'The Body and Blood of Christ' [Corpus Christi].*

🎼 In memory of Jesus; Lord Jesus Christ, you have come to us; The servant king; This is my body

---

The Passover meal is prepared:
Mk 14$^{12-16}$; Mt 26$^{17-19}$; Lk 22$^{7-13}$

The Last Supper:
Jesus foretells the treachery of Judas -
Mk 14^{18}; Mt 26$^{20-25}$; Lk 22$^{21-23}$; Jn 13$^{21-30}$

The first Eucharist/Mass
Mk 14$^{22-25}$; Mt 26$^{26-29}$;
Lk 22$^{14-38}$ (& other teaching)
(Jn 13-17 & 6$^{48-51}$); (1 Cor 11$^{23-27}$)

Jesus foretells Peter's denial
Mk 14$^{26-31}$; Mt 26$^{30-35}$; Lk 22$^{31-34}$; Jn 13$^{36-38}$

The Garden of Gethsemane and the arrest of Jesus
Mk 14$^{32-52}$; Mt 26$^{36-56}$; Lk 22$^{39-53}$; Jn 18$^{1-11}$

The trial before the Jewish leaders
Mk 14$^{53-65}$; Mt 26$^{57-68}$; Lk 22$^{66-71}$; Jn 18$^{12-27}$

Peter's denial
Mk 14$^{66-72}$; Mt 26$^{69-75}$; Lk 22$^{54-62}$; Jn 18$^{15-27}$

GOOD FRIDAY

1   During the time of the Crusades (1095-1270) pilgrims to the Holy Land prayed in Jerusalem as they walked "the Way of the Cross", the route Jesus was thought to have taken on Good Friday.

2   Many people had found it prayerful to follow "the Way of the Cross" in Jerusalem but, when the Moslems re-captured the Holy Land, it became dangerous for Christian pilgrims to visit. From that time, people made a substitute pilgrimage by following in church grounds a set of statues or pictures that brought to mind the journey of Jesus to his death. "Stations of the Cross" (as they tended to be called) began to appear inside churches. Catholic churches now have 14 Stations of the Cross. In church, some people pray privately whilst thinking of one or more of the scenes.

3   These are the 14 scenes or "stations":

1)   Jesus is condemned to death by Pilate.
2)   Jesus takes up his cross.
3)   Jesus falls the first time.
4)   Jesus meets Mary, his Mother.
5)   Simon of Cyrene helps Jesus to carry his cross.
6)   Veronica wipes the face of Jesus.
7)   Jesus falls a second time.
8)   The women of Jerusalem mourn for Jesus.
9)   Jesus falls a third time.
10) Jesus is stripped of his clothes.
11) Jesus is nailed to the cross.
12) Jesus dies on the cross.
13) Jesus is taken down from the cross.
14) Jesus is placed in the tomb.

4   There is a saying:

"If you were brought to trial
for being a Christian,
would there be enough evidence
to convict you?"

We pause for a few moments and reflect and pray...   *(pause...)*

5   Thomas à Kempis wrote a book called *'The Imitation of Christ'*, in which he writes:

"If you bear the cross gladly, it will bear you."

We pause for a moment...   *(pause...)*

6   *Let us pray:*

Lord Jesus, at our baptism
we were marked for you
with the sign of the Cross.
May your cross inspire us
to act justly and love tenderly.
May the crosses in our lives
be for us
invitations for growth and new life
as we place our trust in you.
Renewed by your love,
may the way we live
proclaim you as Lord:
you who are the Way,
the Truth and the Life.
Amen.

7   People who are deaf and who use sign language, gently touch the palms of their hands as they "sign" the name of "Jesus". We pause and reflect and pray... *(pause...)*

8   John XXIII was Pope from 1958 until 1963. He helped to renew the Church for the present times. A few days before he died, Pope John told one of his staff:

"The secret of my ministry
is in that crucifix
you see opposite my bed.
It's there so that I can see it
in my first waking moment
and before going to sleep.
Look at it, see it as I see it.
Those open arms
have been the programme
of all that I have tried to do as Pope:

they say that Christ died for all - for all.
No one is excluded from his love,
from his forgiveness."

Let's pause for a few moments of reflection and prayer…   *(pause…)*

9 Cardinal Newman wrote:

'Let us come into his Presence whenever we can. Let us try to imagine seeing the cross and him upon it. Let us draw near to it. Let us beg him to look on us as he did on the penitent thief, and let us say to him: "Lord, remember me when you come into your kingdom."'

We spend a few moments in reflection and prayer…   *(pause…)*

10 *Let us pray:*

Lord Jesus,
    you shared the depths
    of our human existence,
    and you loved to the extent
    of placing your life
    into the hands of others.
May your Spirit enable us
    to grow in dependence on our Father,
    and live more fully his will for us,
    so that, in difficult times
    as well as in good times,
    we will be able to say to him
    with confidence,
"Father, I place myself into your hands."

11 *On this day we make the Sign of the Cross together, praying that everything we do today we may do*
in the name of the Father,
and of the Son,
and of the Holy Spirit. Amen.

 *The letters "INRI" to be found above many figures of Christ on crucifixes are an abbreviation of the Latin words: "Iesus*

Nazarenus Rex Iudaeorum" - "Jesus of Nazareth, King of the Jews", being the words on the notice that Pilate had nailed to the cross [John 19$^{19-22}$]. Several interpretations can be given to Pilate's action; one is that Pilate was thereby giving a message that the same dreadful punishment would be given to anyone who tried to lead a rebellion.

 *Pilate offered the people a choice between freeing the murderer, Barabbas, whose name means "son of the father", and Jesus, who was Son of God the Father.*

Jesus, remember me (Taizé); My song is love unknown; O sacred head ill-used; The servant king; Were you there when they crucified my Lord?

EARLY MORNING
The trial before Pilate
Mk 15$^{1-15}$; Mt 27$^{1-2, 11-26}$; Lk 23$^{1-25}$ (& before Herod); Jn 18^{28}-19^{16}

The death of Judas
Mt 27$^{3-10}$

Jesus is mocked by the soldiers
Mk 15$^{16-20}$; Mt 27$^{27-31}$; Jn 19$^{23-24}$

The way of the cross
Mk 15$^{21-22}$; Mt 27^{32}; Lk 23$^{26-32}$; Jn 19^{17}

9.00AM
Nailed to the cross
Mk 15$^{23-27}$; Mt 27$^{33-38}$; Lk 23$^{33-34}$; Jn 19$^{18-24}$

MIDDAY
Jesus is mocked on the cross; darkness starts for 3 hours
Mk 15$^{29-32}$; Mt 27$^{39-45}$; Lk 23$^{35-43}$ (& good thief)

3.00PM
Jesus dies on the cross
Mk 15$^{33-41}$; Mt 27$^{46-56}$; Lk 23$^{44-49}$; Jn 19$^{25-37}$

Jesus is taken down and buried
Mk 15$^{42-47}$; Mt 27$^{57-61}$; Lk 23$^{50-56}$; Jn 19$^{38-42}$

Roman soldiers guard the tomb
Mt 27$^{62-66}$

HOLY SATURDAY

1 It was the women who had stayed with Jesus during his 6 hours on the cross; the men ran away. It was the women who took Jesus' body to the tomb.

2 With the Sabbath day starting on the Friday evening (as soon as the first star was visible), there was not enough time to prepare Jesus' body for a proper burial, if "work" was to be avoided on the Sabbath.

3 Throughout Saturday the women waited, ready to return to the tomb on Sunday morning to anoint Jesus' body for a proper burial. The women waited...

4 I think back to times when *I* have waited, felt let down, or been disappointed; times when I have waited for news, have been uncertain about the future, have felt alone, empty, tomb-like. I spend a few moments in silent reflection and prayer, placing all those occasions and my whole life into the hands of God the Father.

5 I ask for the faith to be able to trust and wait...

EASTER SUNDAY

(See also 25 April)

1 From the end of the Second World War in 1945 until 1989, the Communist world and "the West" did a lot to undermine each other, but without actually going to war. It was called "the Cold War".

2 In East Berlin the communist authorities built a giant television broadcasting tower, intending it to be a showpiece, especially as it was close to the border with West Berlin. Near the top of the tower is a revolving restaurant, in the shape of a globe. When the sun shines on it, a large and very bright cross appears on this part of the tower, when viewed from a certain angle. The Communist authorities - who persecuted Christians - were embarrassed that the Christian sign of the cross should be seen on one of their showpiece buildings. They painted over the tower and tried other ways of preventing the cross from shining brilliantly, but it continued to do so, and these days, after the fall of Communism, that cross still shines brightly whenever the sun shines.

3 It's a reminder that the cross of the suffering of Jesus is transformed into the cross of victory over death and suffering and sin.

4 *Let us pray:*

**Lord God, Creator of light,
at the rising of your sun each morning,
let the greatest of all lights
- your love -
rise like the sun
within my heart. Amen.**

📖 *The Jewish sabbath - the holy day and day of rest - is Saturday (starting with sunset on Friday evening). The first Christians chose Sunday as the new sabbath day because on that day Jesus rose from the dead.*

📖 *Easter is celebrated on the first Sunday after the full moon following the vernal equinox.*

📖 *The prayer, "Lord God, Creator of light" is short enough to be learned by heart and often prayed, especially when the shining sun can serve as a reminder of God's radiant love.*

🎼 Alleluia, sing to Jesus; Battle is o'er; Because the Lord is my shepherd; Be not afraid; Bless the Lord, my soul (Taizé); Christ the Lord is risen today; Jesus, you are Lord; Keep in mind; Now the green blade rises; On eagle's wings; Shine, Jesus shine; Surrexit Christus (Taizé); The light of Christ; Thine be the glory; Walk in the light.

> **The tomb is empty -
> "He is risen as he said he would!"**
> *Mk 16; Mt 28; Lk 24; Jn 20-21*

Locating
Bible
Passages

OLD TESTAMENT

Genesis

Gen 1-2 - Creation.
Gen 3 - Fall.
Gen 4 - Cain & Abel.
Gen 6-9 - Flood.
Gen 11 - Babel.
Gen 12-25 - Abraham.
Gen 22 - Isaac: sacrifice.
Gen 25 - Esau & Jacob.
Gen 28 - Jacob's dream.
Gen 32 - Jacob wrestles with God.
Gen 37-50 - Joseph & brothers.

Exodus

Ex 1 - Enslaved.
Ex 2-40 - Moses.
Ex 2 - Moses kills Egyptian.
Ex 3 - Burning bush.
Ex 3-7 - Moses' mission; 'Yahweh'.
Ex 7-12 - 10 plagues.
Ex 12 - Passover.
Ex 14-15 - Crossing the sea.
Ex 16 - Manna.
Ex 17 - Water from the rock.
        Moses raises arms in prayer.
Ex 19-40 - Covenant.
Ex 20 - 10 Commandments = *Deut 5*
Ex 23 - Duties to enemies.
Ex 32 - Golden calf.
Ex 33 - God's glory passes by.
Ex 34 - Moses' face shines.
Ex 40 - Led by cloud & fire.

Leviticus

Lev 26 - I will be your God.

Deuteronomy

Deut 1^{29} - Yahweh has carried you.
Deut 4^{40} - Prosper & live long.
Deut 5 - 10 Commandments = *Ex 20*

Deut 7 - God's blessing.
Deut 8 - Wilderness.
Deut 8-11 - Promised land.
Deut 11 - Write my words on your
        doorpost
Deut 24 - Justice for the poor.
Deut 26 - Offerings.
Deut 30 - Blessing or curse - choose life
        and not death

Joshua

Joshua 6 - Jericho.

Judges

Judges 6-8 - Gideon.
Judges 13-16 - Samson.

Ruth

Ruth 1 - Wherever you go...

1 Samuel

1 Sam 1-2 - Hannah's prayer.
1 Sam 3 - Call of Samuel:
        Speak,Lord,servant listens.
1 Sam 10 - Samuel anoints Saul.
1 Sam 16 - David is anointed.
1 Sam 17 - David & Goliath.
1 Sam 24 - David spares Saul.

2 Samuel

2 Sam 5 - David anointed king.
2 Sam 6 - Ark in Jerusalem.
2 Sam 11 - David & Bathsheba.
2 Sam 12 - Nathan: lamb story.
2 Sam 18-19 - Absalom's death;
        David mourns.

1 Kings

1 Kings 3 - Solomon asks for wisdom.
Solomon's judgement.
1 Kings 10 - Queen of Sheba.
1 Kings 17 - Elijah: flour & oil.
Widow's son raised.
1 Kings 18 - Prophets on Mt Carmel.
1 Kings 19 - Journey to Horeb: "Get up & eat".
Earthquake, wind & fire.
1 Kings 21 - Naboth's vineyard.

2 Kings

2 Kings 2 - Elijah/chariot/whirlwind.
Elisha takes up Elijah's mantle.
2 Kings 4 - Widow's oil.
Elisha raises dead boy.
2 Kings 5 - Naaman's leprosy healed.

1 Chronicles

1 Chron 13 - David & Ark.
1 Chron 29 - David's prayer.

2 Chronicles

2 Chron 1 - Solomon asks for wisdom.
2 Chron 5 - Ark to Temple.
2 Chron 9 - Queen of Sheba.

2 Maccabees

2 Macc 7 - Martyrdom of the 7 brothers.

Job

Job 1,2 - Satan tests Job.

Psalms

Ps 8 - Creation; mankind:
when I see work of your hands.
Ps 22(21) - Why have you forsaken me?
Ps 23(22) - The Lord is my shepherd.
Ps 24(23) - Who shall climb Lord's mountain?
Ps 27(26) - Lord is my light & my help.
Ps 31(30) - Into your hands I commend
my spirit.
Ps 42/43 - Like the deer that yearns.
Ps 51(50) - Have mercy on me in your
kindness
Ps 63(62) - Your love is better than life.
Ps 67(66) - Be gracious and bless us.
Ps 71(70) - Prayer in old age:
In you, Lord, I take refuge.
Ps 84(83) - How lovely is your dwelling
place.
Ps 91(90) - Under the Divine wings:
He who dwells; I will raise you up.
Ps 95(94) - Today listen to his voice.
Ps 100(99) - Enter courts with songs of praise.
Ps 103(102) - My soul, give thanks to the Lord;
the Lord is compassion & love.
Ps 104(103) - Splendour of creation:
Bless the Lord, my soul.
Ps 110(109) - Messiah, King, Priest, Judge.
Ps 112(111) - Good person takes pity and
lends.
Ps 113(112) - From rising of sun to its setting.
From dust he lifts up lowly.
Ps 117(116) - Strong is his love for us.
Ps 118(117) - This is day the Lord has made.
Ps 121(120) - At your right side he stands;
he will guard going and coming.
Ps 122(121) - Let us go to God's house.
Ps 126(125) - Song of the Return.
Ps 127(126) - If Lord does not build house.
Ps 130(129) - Out of the depths I cry to you.
Ps 131(130) - Like a child.
Ps 134(133) - Night prayer: lift up hands.
Ps 136(135) - For his love endures forever.
Ps 137(136) - By the rivers of Babylon.
Ps 138(137) - Your faithfulness & love;
You stretch out hand & save me.
Ps 139(138) - God's presence;
You search me & know me

Ps 145(144) - Lord is kind & full of compassion
Ps 146(145) - Lord gives sight to blind &
          raises up those bowed down.
Ps 147(146) - heals the brokenhearted;
          Binds up all their wounds.
Ps 147B - Praise the Lord, Jerusalem.
Ps 148 - He commanded, they were made:
          fire & hail, snow & mist.

Ecclesiastes

Ecc 3 - A season & time for everything.

Song of Songs

Song 2 - The cry of my beloved.

Wisdom

Wis 3 - The souls of the virtuous are in...
Wis 7 - Respect for wisdom; I prayed &
       understanding was given me.
Wis 11^{23}-1^{22} - You love all that exists...

Sirach (Ecclesiasticus)

Sir 2 - If you aspire to serve the Lord,
      prepare for an ordeal.
Sir 6 - Friendship.
Sir 17 - The wonder of mankind.
Sir 24 - Wisdom: I came forth from...
Sir 39 - His memory will not disappear.
Sir 43 - The splendour of nature.
Sir 44 - Let us praise illustrious men.

Isaiah

Is 1 - Though your sins are like scarlet...
Is 2 - Let's go up to Temple of the Lord that
    he may teach us his ways. = *Mic 4*
Is 6 - Holy, holy.
Is 7^{14} - Sign: maiden will be with child.
Is 9 - The people that walked in darkness...
a child born for us.
Is 11 - A shoot shall spring; wolf with lamb.
Is 25 - Messianic banquet; destroy death
    & wipe away all tears.
Is 35 - Your God is coming;
    eyes of the blind be opened.
Is 40 - Console my people; prepare the way;
    let every valley; walk & never tire;
    creation - majesty of God;
    put out wings like eagles.
Is 42 - Open eyes of blind.
Is 43 - Do not be afraid: called by name;
    no need to recall the past.
Is 49 - Does a woman forget child?
    name on palms of my hands.
Is 50 - A disciple's tongue;
    I offered my back - struck me.
Is 52 - How lovely on the mountains:
    one who brings good news.
Is 53 - Without beauty or majesty we saw
    him; he was pierced for our
    faults; like a lamb to slaughter.
Is 55 - Come to the water;
    word that goes from my mouth
    does not return to me empty.
Is 58 - Liberty to captives, bread to hungry.
Is 61 - Sent me to bring good news to poor,
    liberty to captives.
Is 66 - Rejoice with Jerusalem.

Jeremiah

Jer 1 - Before I formed you in the womb;
    I put my words into your mouth.
Jer 15 - Your word was my delight
    & the joy of my heart.
Jer 20 - You have seduced me, Lord.
Jer 31^{31} - I will make a new covenant
    I will be their God & they my
    people.
    They will all know me.

Ezekiel

Ezek 11 - I'll gather you -scattered; I'll put new
spirit in you; heart of stone/flesh.
Ezek 34 - Shepherding...
Ezek 36 - I will pour clean water over you
& give you new heart/spirit.
Ezek 37 - Dry bones.

Daniel

Dan 33 - young men in furnace.
Dan 5 - Belshazzar's Feast; writing on wall.
Dan 6,14 - Daniel thrown to lions.
Dan 7^{13},10^{16} - "Son of man"
Dan 13 - Susanna; Daniel's judgement.

Hosea

Hos 11 - When Israel was a child I loved him;
the more I called, further they went
from me.
Hos 14 - Come back to the Lord.

Joel

Joel 2 - Come back to me; God is
tenderness & compassion.
Joel 3 - I will pour out my spirit;
young men have visions
& old men have dreams.

Amos

Am 5 - Hate evil, love good;
let justice flow like water, &
integrity like unfailing stream.
Am 7 - Plumb-line.
Am 8 - You who trample on the needy;
tampering with the scales.

Jonah

Jon 1 - Jonah thrown overboard.
Jon 2 - Swallowed by great fish.
Jon 3 - People of Nineveh repent.
Jon 4 - Jonah & castor-oil plant.

Micah

Mic 4 - Let's go up to mountain of Lord
that he may teach us his ways.
= Isaiah 2
Swords into ploughshares.
Nation not lift up sword...
Mic 6 - My people, what have I done to you?
Act justly, love tenderly,
walk humbly with God.
Mic 7^{19} - Tread down our faults;
cast them to bottom of sea.

Habbakuk

Hab 3^{17} - Though fig tree doesn't blossom...
yet I will rejoice in the Lord.

Zephaniah

Zeph 3^{17} - Yahweh is in your midst;
he will renew you by his love.

NEW TESTAMENT- GOSPELS

EVENTS

Early life

Word of Life - Jn 1[1-18]
Genealogy - Mt 1[1-17]; Lk 3[23-38]
Birth & infancy - Mt 1-2; Lk 1-2
John the Baptist - Mt 3[1-12],11[1-15], 14[1-12];
  Mk 1[1-8],6[14-29]; Lk 1,3[1-20],7[18-27];
  Jn 1[19-34],3[22-33]

Early ministry

Baptism of Jesus -Mt 3[13-17]; Mk 1[9-11];
  Lk 3[21-22]
Temptation of Jesus -Mt 3[13-17]; Mk 1[12-13];
  Lk 4[1-13]
In Nazareth synagogue - Lk 4[16-30]
Jesus calls the 12 -Mt 4[18-22],9[9];
  Mk 1[16-20],2[13-14],3[13-19];
  Lk 5[1-11,27-28],6[12-16]; Jn 1[35-51]

Other events

Adulterous woman -Jn 8[1-11]
Cana: wedding -Jn 2[1-12]
Children: example;greatness - Mt 18[1-10],
  19[13-15]; Mk 9[33-37,42-50],10[13-16]; Lk 9[46-48],
  10[21-22],18[15-17]
Cleansing of temple -Mt 21[12-13]; Mk 11[15-17];
  Lk 19[45-46]; Jn 2[13-25]
Eating with sinners - Mt 9[10-13]; Mk 2[13-17];
  Lk 5[29-32]
Martha & Mary -Lk 10[38-42]
Mission of the 12 -Mt 10[1-42]; Mk 6[7-13];
  Lk 9[1-6]
Mission of the 72 -Lk 10[1-12]
Payment of Temple tax -Mt 17[24-27]
Peter's profession of faith -Mt 16[13-20];
  Mk 8[27-30]; Lk 9[18-21]; Jn 6[67-71]
Picking corn on Sabbath - Mt 12[1-8];
  Mk 2[23-28]; Lk 6[1-5]
Rejected at Nazareth - Mt 13[53-58]; Mk 6[1-6];
  Lk 4[16-30]

Rich young man - Mt 19[16-26]; Mk 10[17-27];
  Lk 18[18-30]
Samaritan woman at well - Jn 4[1-42]
Transfiguration - Mt 17[1-8]; Mk 9[2-8]; Lk 9[28-36]
Widow's Mite - Mk 12[41-44]; Lk 21[1-4]
Woman sinner: wipes feet of Jesus - Lk 7[36-50]
Zacchaeus -Lk 19[1-10]

Last days

Entry to Jerusalem - Mt 21[3-11]; Mk 11[1-22];
  Lk 19[28-38]; Jn 12[12-19]
Anointing at Bethany - Mt 26[6-13]; Mk 14[3-9];
  Jn 12[1-8]
Last Supper - Mt 26[17-29]; Mk 14[12-25];
  Lk 22[7-20]; (also 1 Cor 11[23-25])
Gethsemane - Mt 26[36-56]; Mk 14[32-52];
  Lk 22[39-53]; Jn 18[1-11]
Crucifixion & Resurrection - Mt 27-28;
  Mk 15-16; Lk 23-24; Jn 19-21
Emmaus - Lk 24[13-35]
Ascension - Lk 24[50-53] (& ACTS 1[6-11])

JESUS' TEACHING

(in what follows: *italicised* = in Sermon
  on Mount, being Mt 5-7; Lk 6[17-49])

Almsgiving - Mt 6[1-4]
Ask,seek,knock - Mt 7[7-11]; Lk 11[9-13]

Barren fig tree - Mt 21[18-22]; Mk 11[12-25]
Beatitudes - Mt 5[1-12]; Lk 6[20-26]
*'Be compassionate/merciful as your Father
  is' - Lk 6[36-37]*
But I say to you - Mt 5[20-48]

Divorce - Mt 5[31],19[1-9]; Mk 10[1-12]; Lk 16[18]
Do not let your hearts be troubled - Jn 14[1]

Eye - Mt 6[22-23]; Lk 11[34-36]);

Faith - Mt 21[18-22]; (Lk 17[5-6])
*False prophets & true disciples: by their fruit
  - Mt 7[15-27]; Lk 6[43-44];*

PARABLES

Coins: silver/gold (talents) - Mt 25$^{14\text{-}30}$; Lk 19$^{11\text{-}27}$
Counting cost: building & fighting -Lk 14$^{25\text{-}33}$
Crafty steward ("write 50") - Lk 16$^{1\text{-}8}$
Darnel(weeds) - Mt 13$^{24\text{-}30}$
Dragnet - Mt 13$^{47\text{-}50}$
Fig tree (unfruitful) - Lk 13$^{6\text{-}9}$
Good Samaritan - Lk 10$^{29\text{-}37}$
Great feast - Mt 22$^{1\text{-}10}$; Lk 14$^{15\text{-}24}$
Growing seed - Mk 4$^{26\text{-}29}$
Labourers in vineyard - Mt 20$^{1\text{-}16}$
Lamp - Mk 4$^{21\text{-}23}$; Lk 8$^{16\text{-}18}$,11$^{33\text{-}36}$
Lost coin - Lk 15$^{8\text{-}10}$
Lost sheep - Mt 18$^{12\text{-}14}$; Lk 15$^{4\text{-}7}$
Lost son - Lk 15$^{11\text{-}32}$
Measure - Mk 4$^{24\text{-}25}$
Mustard seed - Mt 13$^{31\text{-}32,36\text{-}43}$; Mk 4$^{30\text{-}32}$; Lk 13$^{18\text{-}19}$
New cloth on old coat - Mt 9^{16}; Mk 2^{21}; Lk 5^{36}
New wine in used wineskins -Mt 9^{17}; Mk 2^{22}; Lk 5$^{37\text{-}38}$
Pearl - Mt 13$^{45\text{-}46}$
Pharisee & tax collector - Lk 18$^{9\text{-}14}$
Prodigal son - Lk 15$^{11\text{-}32}$
Rich fool (barns) - Lk 12$^{13\text{-}21}$
Rich man & Lazarus (having died) - Lk 16$^{19\text{-}31}$
Servant's duty ("done no more than duty") - Lk 17$^{7\text{-}10}$
Sower - Mt 13$^{4\text{-}23}$; Mk 4$^{1\text{-}20}$; Lk 8$^{4\text{-}15}$
Talents [silver/gold coins] -Mt 25$^{14\text{-}30}$; Lk 19$^{11\text{-}27}$
Tenants in vineyard (wicked husbandmen) - Mt 21$^{33\text{-}46}$; Mk 12$^{1\text{-}12}$; Lk 20$^{9\text{-}19}$
Ten bridesmaids - Mt 25$^{1\text{-}13}$
Treasure - Mt 13^{45}
Two housebuilders - Mt 7$^{24\text{-}27}$; Lk 6$^{46\text{-}49}$
Two sons - Mt 21$^{28\text{-}32}$
Unforgiving debtor - Mt 18$^{23\text{-}35}$
Unfruitful fig tree - Lk 13$^{6\text{-}9}$
Watchful servants - Lk 12$^{35\text{-}48}$
Wedding feast (man without wedding clothes) - Mt 22$^{1\text{-}14}$
Widow & Judge - Lk 18$^{1\text{-}8}$
Wise & faithful steward - Mt 24$^{45\text{-}51}$
Yeast - Mt 13^{33}; Lk 13$^{20\text{-}21}$

MIRACLES

People-miracles

Blind man at Bethsaida - Mk 8$^{22\text{-}26}$
Blind man/men of Jericho - Mt 20$^{29\text{-}34}$; Mk 10$^{46\text{-}52}$; Lk 18$^{35\text{-}43}$
Centurion's servant - Mt 8$^{5\text{-}13}$; Lk 7$^{1\text{-}10}$
Crippled woman on Sabbath - Lk 13$^{10\text{-}17}$
Daughter of Canaanite/Syrophoenician woman healed - Mt 15$^{21\text{-}28}$; Mk 7$^{24\text{-}30}$
Deaf & dumb man - Mk 7$^{31\text{-}37}$
Demoniac - Mk 1$^{21\text{-}28}$; Lk 4$^{31\text{-}37}$
Demoniac, pigs - Mt 8$^{28\text{-}34}$; Mk 5$^{1\text{-}20}$; Lk 8$^{26\text{-}39}$
Dropsical man on Sabbath - Lk 14$^{1\text{-}6}$
Dumb demoniac - Mt 9$^{32\text{-}34}$
Ear of High Priest's slave - Lk 22$^{50\text{-}51}$
Epileptic demoniac - Mt 17$^{14\text{-}20}$; Mk 9$^{14\text{-}29}$; Lk 9$^{37\text{-}43}$
Jairus' daughter raised to life - Mt 9$^{18\text{-}36}$; Mk 5$^{21\text{-}43}$; Lk 8$^{40\text{-}56}$
Lazarus raised - Jn 11
Leper - Mt 8$^{1\text{-}4}$; Mk 1$^{40\text{-}45}$; Lk 5$^{12\text{-}16}$
Man born blind - Jn 9
Official's son in Capernaum ("Go: your son will live") - Jn 4$^{43\text{-}54}$
Paralytic - Mt 9$^{1\text{-}8}$; Mk 2$^{1\text{-}12}$; Lk 5$^{17\text{-}26}$
Sick touch fringe of cloak - Mt 14$^{34\text{-}36}$
Sick man at Sheep Pool in Jerusalem - Jn 5$^{1\text{-}18}$
Simon Peter's mother-in-law - Mt 8$^{14\text{-}15}$; Mk 1$^{29\text{-}31}$; Lk 4$^{38\text{-}39}$
Ten lepers - Lk 17$^{11\text{-}19}$
Two blind men - Mt 9$^{27\text{-}31}$
Widow of Nain's son raised - Lk 7$^{11\text{-}17}$
Withered hand - Mt 12$^{9\text{-}14}$; Mk 3$^{1\text{-}6}$; Lk 6$^{6\text{-}11}$
Woman with haemorrhage - Mt 9$^{18\text{-}26}$; Mk 5$^{21\text{-}43}$; Lk 8$^{40\text{-}56}$

Nature-miracles

Calming of storm - Mt 8$^{23\text{-}27}$; Mk 4$^{35\text{-}41}$; Lk 8$^{22\text{-}25}$
Cana: water into wine - Jn 2$^{1\text{-}11}$
Catches of fish - Lk 5$^{1\text{-}11}$; and Jn 21$^{1\text{-}11}$
Feeds 4000 - Mt 15$^{32\text{-}39}$; Mk 8$^{1\text{-}10}$
Feeds 5000 - Mt 14$^{13\text{-}21}$; Mk 6$^{30\text{-}44}$; Lk 9$^{10\text{-}17}$; Jn 6$^{1\text{-}15}$
Walks on water - Mt 14$^{22\text{-}33}$; Mk 6$^{45\text{-}52}$; Jn 6$^{16\text{-}21}$

NEW TESTAMENT- ACTS, LETTERS

ACTS

Acts 1^{6-11} - Ascension (& Lk 24^{50-53})

Acts 2 - Pentecost.

Acts 2^{42-47} - Early Christian community: faithful to teaching, brotherhood, breaking of bread.

Acts 3 - Cure of cripple:"Neither silver/ gold".

Acts 4^{32-35} - Early Christian community

Acts 5^{12-16} - Signs & wonders; shadow of Peter.

Acts 5^{22-33} - Obedience to God/men

Acts 5^{34-42} - Gamaliel: if of human origin/if from God.

Acts 6^{1-7}-7 - helpers.

Acts 6^{8}-8^{3} - Stephen's death; "Saul approved".

Acts 8^{9-25} - Simon the magician: simony.

Acts 9^{1-31} - Conversion of Saul (Paul): (Paul's own account: 22^{6-21}, 26^{12-18}; Gal 1^{11}-2^{10})

Acts 9^{36-43} - Tabitha raised to life in Jaffa.

Acts 10^{1}-11^{8}- Centurion Cornelius & Peter's Dream: God has no favourites (& 11^{1-18}; Gal 2^{6}).

Acts 11^{26} - At Antioch: first called Christians.

Acts 12^{1-19} - Peter's arrest & deliverance: angel.

Acts 13^{4-12} - Fraudulent Elymas is blinded.

Acts 14^{8-18} - Cripple healed: Paul & Barnabas about to be worshipped.

Acts 16^{16-40}- Miraculous deliverance of Paul & Silas: earthquake; gaoler converted.

Acts 17^{28} - In him we live & move & have our being.

Acts 20^{7-12} - Eutychus falls from window; raised to life.

Acts 20^{35} - "More happiness in giving than receiving."

LETTERS

Romans

Rom 5^{1-11} - Faith guarantees salvation; sufferings bring patience, perseverance, hope; Christ died for us while we were still sinners.

Rom 6^{5-11} - Having died with Christ we shall return to life with him. Dead to sin; alive to God.

Rom 7^{14-25} - I fail to carry out what I want to do.

Rom 8^{1-11} - No condemnation for those in Jesus Christ.

Rom 8^{14-17} - Moved by Spirit: 'Abba, Father'. Heirs of God, sharing Christ's sufferings.

Rom 8^{18-27} - What we suffer in this life. Freeing of all creation. Spirit helps us in our weakness.

Rom 8^{28-30} - God turns everything to their good.

Rom 8^{31-39} - With God on our side, could anyone condemn? Nothing can come between us & Christ's love. Trials through which we triumph. Neither death nor life....

Rom 10^{9-13} - If you confess that Jesus is Lord...

Rom 11^{33-36} - How rich are depths of God.

Rom 12^{3-13} - If your gift is...then use it. Don't let love be a pretence. Don't give up if trials come. Make hospitality special care.

Rom 12^{14-21}- Bless those who persecute you. Resist evil & conquer with good.

Rom 13^{1-7} - Obey civil authority.

Rom 13^{8-10}- Debt of mutual love.

Rom 14^{7-12}- Life & death of each of us has its influence on others. If we live, we live for the Lord.

1 Corinthians

1 Cor 1^{17-31} - Cross is illogical to....
1 Cor 3^{5-15} - Fellow-workers with God; foundation is Jesus.
1 Cor 3^{16-17} - You are God's temple.
1 Cor 4^{10} - Fools for Christ; scum of earth.
1 Cor 9^{22} - All things to all men.
1 Cor 11^{20-27} - The Lord's Supper.
1 Cor 12^{1-31} - Variety of gifts; same Spirit; analogy of the body.
1 Cor $12^{31}-14^{1}$ - LOVE is...
1 Cor 15 - Resurrection; perishable nature; Death: victory? Sting? By God's grace I am what I am.

2 Corinthians

2 Cor 1^{1-11} - God comforts us that we may comfort others.
2 Cor 3 - You are letter from Christ/Spirit.
2 Cor 3^{18} - With unveiled faces we reflect God's brightness, & are turned into image we reflect.
2 Cor 4 - Not ourselves we preach. We are earthenware jars; power comes from God.
2 Cor 5^{16-21} - God reconciled us to himself. In Christ we are a new creation. Ambassadors for Christ.
2 Cor 6^{3-10} - Fortitude in times of suffering; said to be dying & here are alive; with nothing, though everything.
2 Cor 7^{10} - To suffer in God's way.
2 Cor 9^{6-15} - Thin sowing/reaping.
2 Cor $11^{21}-12^{12}$ - God's grace enough for you; his power best in weakness. Paul's own sufferings. When weak then I am strong.

Galatians

Gal 2^{11-14} - Paul disagrees with Peter.
Gal 2^{19-20} - I've been crucified with Christ & live now with Christ's life.
Gal 4^{1-7} - God sent his Son,born of woman. Spirit cries 'Abba, Father': you are a son & heir.
Gal 5 - Christian freedom in Spirit. Love, joy, peace, patience....

Ephesians

Eph 1 - Blessed be God and Father....
Eph 2^{1-10} - God loved us with so much love; how infinitely rich in grace. Saved by grace, through faith. We are God's work of art.
Eph 3^{14-21} - Out of his infinite glory, may he give you...power to grow strong; planted in love; breadth, length...
Eph 4^{1-8} - Worthy of your vocation. One Lord/faith/baptism... Varied gifts for Body of Christ: to be apostles, prophets, teachers...
Eph 4^{17-32} - Give up old way of life; spiritual revolution; put on new self.
Eph 6^{10-20} - Put on God's armour.

Philippians

Phil 2^{1-11} - Jesus didn't cling to his equality, but emptied himself.
Phil 2^{12-18} - God puts will & action into you. Shine in world like bright stars: you are offering it the word of life.
Phil 3^{6-14} - I look on everything as rubbish if I can know Christ & power of resurrection. I run the race...
Phil 4^{4-9} - I want you to be happy in Lord. Fill your minds with everything that's true,noble,good,pure.

Colossians

Col 1 13-20 - Taken us out of power of
darkness & created a place
for us in Kingdom.
He is image of invisible God...
Col 1 24-29 - Servant of the Church.
Mystery is Christ among you.
I struggle wearily on: his
power drives me irresistibly.
Col 3 5-17 - You have put on a new self.
God's chosen race -he loves you.
Bear with one another.
Let Christ's message find
home in you.
Col 3 24 - It is Christ that you are
serving.

1 Thessalonians

1 Thess 4 13-5 11 - Those who have died.
Children of light;
Lord's Day.
1 Thess 5 12-22 - Be happy. Pray constantly.
Give thanks.

2 Thessalonians

2 Thess 3 6-15 - Some living in idleness;
give no food to those who
refuse to work.

1 Timothy

1 Tim 4 12-16 -Don't let people disregard
you because you are young;
use your spiritual gifts.
1 Tim 6 11-14 -Your aims & fight good fight.

2 Timothy

2 Tim 1 6-9 - Fan into a flame God's gifts.
2 Tim 2 1-13 -If we have died with him...
He is faithful.

2 Tim 3 1-5 - Outward appearance of
religion; inner power.
2 Tim 4 1-5 - Refute falsehood, shun novelties.
2 Tim 4 6-8 - I have fought the good fight

Philemon

Philem 1 1-25 - Runaway slave.

Hebrews

Heb 1 1-4 - At various times in past, God
spoke... but now through his
Son, who is radiant light
of God's glory.
Heb 5 1-10 - He offered up prayer &
entreaty. Although Son,
obeyed through suffering.
Heb 11 1-40 - FAITH of our ancestors...
Heb 12 1-4 - Many witnesses in cloud
around us.
Heb 13 1 - Welcome strangers (are angels?)

James

Jas 1 1-7 - Be happy when trials come.
Jas 1 22-27 - Hearers & do-ers: putting
word into practice.
Jas 2 1-13 - Respect for the poor.
Jas 2 12-26 - Faith & good works.
Jas 5 13-18 - Anointing of the sick.

1 Peter

1 Pet 1 3-9 - Faith tested like gold.
You didn't see him, yet love him.
1 Pet 2 9-10 - Chosen race,royal priesthood,
consecrated nation,people
apart.
1 Pet 2 17 - Respect God; honour Emperor.
1 Pet 2 18-24 - Christ suffered for you:
example. By his wounds you
are healed.

1 Pet 3^9 - Pay back with a blessing.
1 Pet 4^{7-11} - Each has received special grace.
1 Pet 4^{12-19} - Suffering as Christians.
1 Pet 5^{5-11} - Unload all your worries; devil prowling around.

2 Peter

2 Pet 3^{8-10} - With Lord 1 day = 1000 years

1 John

1 Jn 1^{1-3} - We have seen & touched the Word who is life.
1 Jn 1^{5-7} - God is light.
1 Jn 1^{8-10} - If we say we've no sin in us...
1 Jn 3^1 Think of the love the Father has lavished on us.
1 Jn 4^{7-21} - God is love: God loved us first.
1 Jn 4^{18} - Perfect love drives out fear.

REVELATION

Rev 1^{4-8} - Washed away our sins with his blood: we're kings & priests.
Alpha & Omega (+ 21^6,22^{13})
Rev 3^{14-22} - I stand at door & knock.
Rev 5^{9-13} - Worthy to take scroll. Power,riches,wisdom,strength.
Rev 7^{9-17} - Huge number: persecuted are in washed robes.
Rev 12^{1-17} - Sign: pregnant woman; dragon.
Rev 14^{13-20} - On dying. Angel; sickle.
Rev 15^{3-4} - Great & wonderful your works.
Rev 19^{5-10} - Wedding-feast of the Lamb.
Rev 21^{1-8} - New heaven & new earth. Here God lives among men. He will wipe away all tears.
Rev 22^2 - Leaves of tree for healing of nations.
Rev 22^{17} - Spirit & Bride say: 'Come'. All who are thirsty: 'Come'.

Index

INDEX

Costner, Kevin - 5 March
Coubertin, Pierre de - 6 April
Country - 20 Jan
Courage - 12 Jan; 4 March; 15 Feb
Creation - 8 Jan, 12 Feb; 1,8,31 March;
    11,12,13 April
Cricket - 15 March
Cross - Good Friday & Easter Sunday, Vol 1
Crucifix - 26 March
Crusades - Good Friday, Vol 1
Cuba - 18 Jan
Cunard - 22 Jan

Dachau - 22 March
Damian, Fr - 19 March
Darkness - 1 Jan, 3 April
Darwin, Charles - 12 Feb
David, St - 1 March
Da Vinci, Leonardo - Maundy Thursday, Vol 1
Dead Poets' Society - 7 Jan
Deafness - see 'Helen Keller';
    Good Friday, Vol 1
Death - 23 Jan; 7 Feb; 21,24 March;
    5,8,14,15 April
Decimal currency - 10 Jan
De La Salle, John Baptist - 7 April
Diamond (dog) - 20 March
Dickens, Charles - Intro
Differences - 8 Feb
Discrimination - see 'prejudice'
Dog - 20 March
Door - 1 Jan, 26 Feb
Dream - 4 April
Dunblane - 3 March
Dying - see 'Death'

Education Reform Act - Intro
Egypt - 16 Feb
Einstein, Albert - 14 March; 18 April
Election - 20 Jan
Electricity - 3 Feb
Elijah - Shrove Tuesday, Vol 1
Eliot, TS - 7 Jan; Shrove Tuesday, Vol 1
Elizabeth I, Queen - 23 March

Elizabeth II, Queen - 20 April; Maundy
    Thursday, Vol 1
Emerson, RW - 5 Feb
Emmaus - Intro
Enemies - 15 Jan
Encourage - 27 Jan
Epiphany - 5,6,7 Jan
Evolution - 12 Feb

Failure - 4 March; see also 'success'
Fairtrade - 10 April
Faithfulness - 13 Feb; 20 March
Fear - 28 Feb
Fire - 26 Feb; 20 March
Fleming, Dr Alexander - 9 Jan; 11 March
Flowers - 15 April
Food - 16 March
Football - 13 Jan; 29 March; 29 April
Forgiveness - 17 Jan; 26 Feb; 23 March
Francis of Assisi - 5 March
Frank, Anne - 12 March
Frankincense - 7 Jan
Franklin, Benjamin - 17 April
Freeman, Laurence - Intro
Friends - 23 April

Gagarin, Yuri - 12 April
Galileo - 8 Jan
Gandhi - 29,30 Jan; 5,17 Feb
General Election - 20 Jan
Genesis - 12 Feb
George, St - 23 April
George VI, King - 1,22 Jan
Gifts - 5,6,7,20 Jan
Glencoe - 13 Feb
Gold - 5,7 Jan
Gospel - 17 Feb
Grahame, Kenneth - 8 March
Gravitation - 4 Jan
Great Fire of London - 26 Feb
Gregory XIII, Pope - 4 Jan
Grellet, Stephen - 11 March
Griffiths, Bede - Intro
Grimm, Brothers - Intro

Hale-Bopp Comet - 13 April
Halley's Comet - 13 April
Harriot, John - Intro
Harvey, Dr William - 1 April
Haskins, Minnie - 1 Jan
Hatred - 4 Feb
Hawaii - 19 March
Heart - 1 April
Healing - 11 Feb
Heaven - 16 April
Hell - 16 April
Henry VIII, King - 7 Feb
Hill, Rowland - 10 Jan
Hillsborough - 15 April
Hitler, Adolf - 22 Jan; 4 Feb; 30 April
Hoffman, Felix - 6 March
Hostages - 24 Jan
Hunger - 16 March; Family Fast Day

Ideals - 12 March
Ignatius Loyola - 5 Feb
Illness - 11 Feb, 6 March
Incense - 7 Jan
Individuality - 10,22 Jan; 3,29 March;
    7,29 April
Initiative - 20 Jan
INRI - Good Friday, Vol 1
Ireland - 17 March
Isaiah 2 - 27 Feb
Islam - 24 Feb; 30 March; 19 April

Jail - 5 Feb
James II, King - 13,26 Feb
Janus - 1 Jan
John, Brother - 8 April
John Paul II, Pope - Intro; 11 Feb
John XXIII, Pope - 18 Jan; Good Friday, Vol 1
Jonah - 2 March; Shrove Tuesday, Vol 1
Journey - 11 Jan; Palm Sunday, Vol 1;
    Good Friday, Vol 1
Judaism -30 March
Judas - Maundy Thursday, Vol 1
Judging - 1 Feb; 22 March; 4,27 April

Jupiter - 8 Jan
Justice - 15 Jan; 5,20 Feb; 18,21,24 March;
    Family Fast Day, Vol 1

Kennedy, JF - 20 Jan
King, Martin Luther - 15 Jan; 4,5 April
Khrushchev - 18 Jan
Knowledge - 4 Jan
Koran - 19 April
Korea - 16 April

Lebanon - 24 Jan
Lent - Volume 1
Leonardo da Vinci - Maundy Thursday, Vol 1
Lepers - 19 March
Light - 1 Jan; 2 Feb
Lincoln, Abraham - 4 March; 9 April
Liverpool - 8,9 Feb; 15 April
London - 11 Jan; 26 Feb
Lourdes - 11 Feb
Love - 14 Feb
Lowry, LS - 23 Feb
Loyalty - 13 Feb
Loyola, St Ignatius - 31 March

Magee, John - 28 Jan
Malta - 25 Jan
Manchester United - 6 Feb
Mandela, Nelson - Intro; 27 April
Marconi - 27 March
Mardi Gras - Shrove Tuesday, Vol 1
Mark, St - 25 April
Mary (Our Lady) - 2,11,28 Feb; 25 March
Mary, Queen - 22 Jan
Masefield, John - 12 Jan
Memories - 5 Jan
Micah 4 - 27 Feb; 22 April
Michelangelo - 18 Feb
Molokai - 19 March
Monument - 26 Feb
Moon - 11,12 April
Moonlight Sonata - 3 March
More, St Thomas - 7 Feb
Morse Code - 14 April

Moses - Shrove Tuesday, Vol 1
Music - 3 March
Myrrh - 6,7 Jan
Name - 22 Jan; 23 Feb; 7,29 April
Napoleon - 17 Jan
National Anthem - 20 April
Nazis - 22 March
New Orleans - Shrove Tuesday, Vol 1
Newman, JH - 21 Feb; Good Friday, Vol 1
Newton, Sir Isaac - 4 Jan; 20 March
New Year - 1, 16 Jan
Nineveh - 2 March
Noah - Shrove Tuesday, Vol 1
Nobel Prize - 14 Jan
Nolan, Chris - 19 Jan

Offertory prayers - 30 March
Olympic Games - 6 April
Only Fools and Horses - 3 Feb
Opportunities - 9 Jan
Our Lady - see 'Mary'

Pain - 6 Jan - see also 'illness'
Pancakes - Shrove Tuesday, Vol 1
Paris - 26 March
Parks, Rosa - 15 Jan
Parliament - 7 Feb
Patrick, St - 17 March
Paul, Saint - 25,26,27 Jan
Paul VI, Pope - Intro
Peace - 23 Jan; 27 Feb; 5,13 March; 9 April
    see also 'Justice'
Penicillin - 9 Jan
Penn, William - 5 March
Pentecost - 18 Jan
Peter, St - 28 Feb
Peter Pan - 22 Feb
Philippians 4 - 22 Feb
Philosophers - 5,20 Feb
Pilgrim's Progress - 24 Jan
Plato - Intro
Positive - 18 Feb
Poverty - Family Fast Day, Vol 1
Prejudice - 15,29 Jan; 21 March; 4,30 April

Presence of God - 10,24,25 Feb; 17,26,
    27,31 March; 1,7,12,22,25 April
Presentation - 2 Feb
President - 20 Jan
Priorities - Family Fast Day, Vol 1
Prodigal Son - Intro, Shrove Tuesday, Vol 1
Prophet - 2 March, 22 April
Psalm 8 - 12 April
Psalm 117 - 20 April
Psalm 137 - 25 Feb
Psalms 138/9 - 10,25 Feb
Pullias - Intro

Quakers - 24 Jan, 5 March
Qualities - see 'talents'
Qur'an - 19 April

Radiation - 26 April
Radio - 27 March
Ravensbruck - 22 March
Reagan, Presd. Ronald - 28 Jan
Reconciliation - 26 March;
    Shrove Tuesday, Vol 1
Responsibilities - 20 Jan; 26 April
Rheumatism - 6 March
Richard of Chichester - 2 April
Rio de Janeiro - Shrove Tuesday, Vol 1
Romans 12 - 26 Jan
Rome - 1 Jan
Romero, Oscar - 24 March
Röntgen, William - 10 Feb
Rousseau, JJ - 20 Feb

Sacrifice - 30 Jan
Saul - see 'Paul'
Schweitzer, Dr Albert - 14 Jan
Scott, Sir Giles Gilbert - 8,9 Feb
Second Vatican Council - 19 Jan
Second World War - Easter Sunday, Vol 1
Seeing - see 'blindness' and 'vision'
Segregation - see 'apartheid', 'prejudice'
Self-esteem - 22 Jan; 23 Feb; 29 April
Shackleton, Ernest - 15 Feb
Shakespeare - 6 Jan; 20 March; 23 April

Sharing - Family Fast Day, Vol 1
Sharpeville - 21 March
Shaw, Percy - 3 April
Ship - 12,22 January
Shoemaker-Levy Comet - 8 Jan
Sickness - see 'illness'
Sight - see 'blindness' and 'seeing' and 'vision'
Simeon - 2 Feb
Simon Peter - 28 Feb
Sinfulness - Shrove Tuesday, Vol 1
Sistine Chapel - 18 Feb
Slaves - 9 April
Socrates, 1 Feb
Solomon - 4 Jan
Sorrow - 6 Jan
South Africa - 21 March; 27 April
South Pole - 15 Feb
Space - 8,28 Jan; 31 March; 11,12 April
Sport - 13 Jan; 29 March; 29 April
Spring - 1 March
Stamps - 10 Jan
Stars - 31 March
Stations of the Cross - Good Friday, Vol 1
Statue - 13 March
St Helena (island) - 26 Feb
Success - 4 March; 6 April
Suffering - 6 Jan
Sun - 9 March; Easter Sunday, Vol 1

Talents - 9,13 Jan; 9 Feb; 18 April
Telephone - 8 Feb, 10 March
Teresa, Mother - 9 Feb; 4 March
Teresa of Avila - 28 March
Thanksgiving/thankfulness - 9 Feb; 23 April
Thoreau - 5 Feb
Time - 9 Jan; 23 March; 1 April
Titanic - 14 April
Tolpuddle - 18 March
Toothache - 6 Jan
'Touching hearts' - Intro
Trade Unions - 18 March
Train - 3 Jan
Tutankhamen - 16 Feb
Twain, Mark - 27 Jan; 1,21 April

Umbrella - 21 Jan
Underground - 11 Jan
Underhill, Evelyn - Intro
Understanding - 4 Jan
United Nations - 27 Feb
Unity - 18,25 Jan; 8 Feb

Valentine, St - 14 Feb
Values - 7 Feb
Vatican Council, Second - 18 Jan
Venice - 25 April
Victoria, Queen - 21,22 Jan
Virgin Mary - see 'Mary'
Vision - 2 Jan; 1,16,18 Feb; 3 April
    see also 'sight' and 'blindness'
Voltaire - 20 Feb
Voyager - 8 Jan

Waite, Terry - 24 Jan
Walker, Peter - Intro
War - see "Second W.W"; 17,23,28 Jan; 27 Feb;
    13 March; 9,30 April
Waterloo - 17 Jan
Wellington - 17 Jan
Whale - 2 March
Wheat - 19 Feb, 16 March
William III, King - 13 Feb
Wind in Willows, The - 8 March
Wine - 30 March
Wisdom - 4,7,9 Jan
Witness - 17 Feb
Wonder - 8 Jan; 10,16 Feb;
    14 March; 11,12,13 April
World - 29 March
Work - 11 Jan
Wren, Sir Christopher - 26 Feb

X-rays - 10 Feb

Year - 1,16 Jan

Zacchaeus - 23 Feb, 29 April